ANYTHING
THAT'S PEACEFUL

Books by Leonard E. Read

Romance of Reality (1937)
Pattern for Revolt (1948)
Outlook for Freedom (1951)
Government: An Ideal Concept (1954)
Why Not Try Freedom? (1958)
Elements of Libertarian Leadership (1962)
Anything That's Peaceful (1964)
The Free Market and Its Enemy (1965)
Deeper Than You Think (1967)
Accent on the Right (1968)
The Coming Aristocracy (1969)
Let Freedom Reign (1969)
Talking to Myself (1970)
Then Truth Will Out (1971)
To Free or Freeze (1972)
Instead of Violence (1973)
Who's Listening? (1973)
Having My Way (1974)
Castles in the Air (1975)
The Love of Liberty (1975)
Comes the Dawn (1976)
Awake for Freedom's Sake (1977)
Vision (1978)
Liberty: Legacy of Truth (1978)
The Freedom Freeway (1979)
Seeds of Progress (1980)
Thoughts Rule the World (1981)
How Do We Know? (1981)
The Path of Duty (1982)

The Foundation is carrying small supplies of every title: $9.95 each as long as the supply lasts.

ANYTHING
THAT'S PEACEFUL

The Case for the Free Market

LEONARD E. READ

The Foundation for Economic Education, Inc.
Irvington-on-Hudson, New York   1992

About the Author and Publisher

Long before Leonard E. Read (1898–1983) authored this book, he created The Foundation for Economic Education, which is the publisher of this volume. He was convinced that every generation must defend its freedom anew against the intellectual forces that seek through ever new devices to enslave it. Therefore, he dedicated his great strength and ability to the study and dissemination of freedom ideas. He founded the Foundation in 1946 and managed it until his death in 1983.

The Foundation publishes THE FREEMAN, an award-winning monthly journal. It pursues an active Op-Ed program which results in thousands of newspaper editorials. It publishes an unending stream of books and pamphlets. It conducts seminars at FEE headquarters and throughout the country. The Foundation in cooperation with other colleges and universities also offers college courses and tutorial services leading to higher academic degrees.

The Foundation for Economic Education, Inc., is a 26 USC 501 (c) (3) organization. Contributions to FEE are deductible from taxable income.

Originally published September 1964. Reprinted, with a new foreword, October 1992.

FOREWORD

A wise man may at times be angry with the world, or may be grieving for it. But he does not retreat from it in despair, nor does he condemn it. He observes and studies the world, he may explore it and use it, mindful of man's noblest task, to make it better.

Leonard Read performed his duties in this world. The spirit of liberty needed to be rekindled, virtuous liberty, which is the right of doing all the good in man's power, according to God's laws. To this end Leonard Read devoted his life.

"What is man's earthly purpose?" he asked in *Anything That's Peaceful,* which probably is the greatest of his 29 books. "It is to expand one's own consciousness into as near a harmony with Infinite Consciousness as it is within the power of each, or, in more lay terms, to see how nearly one can come to a realization of those creative potentialities peculiar to one's own person, each of us being different in this respect."

Surely Leonard Read's own consciousness approached the perfect harmony he sought. He achieved the complete realization of his creative potentialities.

Leonard Read created a "home" for the friends of freedom everywhere. When pessimism was rife and freedom was engulfed by hostile forces, he built The Foundation for Economic Education on a solid foundation and made it the training ground for a new generation of teachers and scholars. He established an educational organization that withstood the test of time and faces the future with confidence. But above all, in more than three decades he sustained the philosophy of freedom through his prolific writing, through seminars for students, businessmen, and professional people, and through contacts with schools and colleges that sought his guidance.

Leonard was a pathfinder for freedom who carried his spirit into daily action. In *Anything That's Peaceful*, it was his aim to gather the various aspects of his teaching, thinking, and writing into an "integrated, free market theme."

In making available this new edition of *Anything That's Peaceful*, The Foundation for Economic Education seeks to keep the candle burning which Leonard Read lit so many years ago. May it continue to shed some light on the great issues of our time.

—HANS F. SENNHOLZ, *President*

CONTENTS

When the individual forsakes or has taken from him
a sense of self-responsibility, he loses the very essence
of his being.

Socialism gives rise to unnatural and unmarketable
human efforts and specialties, exchangeable only under
duress. If this persists, our once dynamic economy
will spin apart!

Labor unions cause inflation precisely as do chambers
of commerce and all other groups which seek handouts
from the federal treasury; not, as is commonly supposed, by way of price and wage "spirals."

Committees tend to absolve individuals from personal
responsibility for positions taken, thus permitting care-
less and irresponsible actions which seriously threaten
the peace.

Voting presupposes a choice. Citizens have no moral
obligation to cast a ballot for the "lesser of two evils,"
or for one of two trimmers; trimming is not comparative, since every trimmer is without integrity.

*Many favor peace but not many favor
the things that make for peace.*

—THOMAS A KEMPIS

CHAPTER 1

A BREAK WITH
PREVAILING FAITH

GALILEO WAS CALLED on the carpet, tried by the Inquisition, and put in prison because he affirmed the theory of Copernicus that the solar system does not revolve around our earth. The truth as he perceived it was a break with the prevailing faith; he committed the unpardonable sin of affronting the mores. This was his guilt.

Americans—enlightened as we suppose ourselves to be—are inclined to view with scorn that illiberal attitude of some three centuries ago which sought to keep the light of new evidence away from the fallacies of that time. Fie on such childish intolerance; *we* are not afraid of truth; let the light shine in!

Perhaps we should pause for a moment and carefully scrutinize what our own mirror reveals. A letter in the morning mail highlights my point: this woman had visited the librarian of the high school to which she had made a gift of *The Freeman,* a monthly journal that presents, dispassionately but consistently, the rationale of the free market, private property, limited government philosophy, along

with its moral and spiritual antecedents. She discovered
that the journal was not among the periodicals displayed
for student perusal, that it had been discreetly relegated to
the teachers' reading room. What was the reason for this
under-the-rug procedure? The librarian explained, *"The
Freeman* is too conservative."* My correspondent, distraught
by this illiberal attitude—by this attempt to keep students
from knowing about the freedom philosophy—asked of
me, "What can we do about this?"

The answer to this question is to be found in an old
English proverb, "Truth will out!" As it did with Galileo's
theory, so it will do with the ideology of freedom! However,
if we would conserve our energies and act in the best
interests of the freedom philosophy, we will do well to reflect on the most effective way to lend a hand to the philosophy. Suppose, for instance, Galileo had exerted pressure on the Inquisitors to purvey that fragment of truth
he had come upon. The folly of such a tactic is clear: His
truth in the hands of his enemies; heaven forbid! Likewise,
it is folly for us to exert influence on those of the collectivistic faith—be they librarians, teachers, book reviewers or
bookstore owners, politicians, or whoever—to carry the message of individuality and its essential concomitant, freedom
in exchange. If one wishes to win, never choose teammates who are intent on losing the contest. Indeed, such
folks should be scrupulously avoided as partners.

The way to give truth a hand is to pursue a do-it-your-
self policy. Each must do his own seeking and revealing.
Such success as one experiences will uncover and attract all
the useful, helpful, sympathetic teammates one's pursuit

deserves. This appears to be truth's obstacle course—no short cuts allowed.

A Dark Age is followed by an Enlightenment; devolution and evolution follow on each other's heels; myth and truth have each their day, now as ever. These opposites—action and reaction—occur with the near regularity of a pendulum, here as elsewhere, the vaunted "common sense of the American people" notwithstanding.

The Faith in Collectivism

Our time, as did Galileo's, witnesses an enormous intolerance toward ideas which challenge the prevailing faith, that faith today being collectivism—world-wide. Americans during the past three or four decades have swung overwhelmingly toward the myths implicit in statism; but, more than this, they have become actually antagonistic to, and afraid of identification with, free market, private property, limited government principles. Indeed, such is the impact of the collectivistic myth, they shy away from any idea or person or institution which the political welfarists and planners choose to label as "rightists." I have labored full time in this controversy for more than thirty years and, having a good memory, these shifts are as clear to me as if they had occurred in the last few moments, or I'd just viewed a time-lapse movie of these events. Were I unaware that such actions and reactions are inevitable in the scheme of things—particularly when observing such behavior by businessmen as well as by teachers, clergymen, and labor officials—I would be unable to believe my eyes.

Yet, truth will out! While myth and truth contend in their never-ending fray, truth inches ahead over the millennia as might be expected from the evolutionary process. My faith says that this is ordained, *if we be worthy,* for what meaning can truth have except our individual perception of it? This is to say that among the numerous imperatives of truth is that many individuals do their utmost in searching for it and reporting whatever their search reveals.

Worthiness also requires of those who would don her mantle a quality of character which I shall call incorruptibility. The more individuals in whom this quality finds refinement the better, and the sooner more truth will out. This quality is too important to suffer neglect for brevity's sake; so let me spell it out.

If my claim for incorruptibility is to hold water, the notion of corruption will have to be refined beyond its generally accepted identification with bribery, stealing, bold-faced lying, and the like. Deplorable as are these specimens, they wreak but minor havoc compared to the more subtle corruptions of the intellect and the soul which, unfortunately, are rarely thought of—or even felt—as corruption.

The level of corruption I wish to examine was suggested to me by a friend's honest confession, "I am as much corrupted by my loves as by my hates." Few of us have succeeded in rising above this weakness; indeed, it is difficult to find *one* who has. Where is the individual who has so freed himself from his affections for or prejudices against persons, parties, creeds that he can utterly disregard these passions and weigh each and every act or proposal or idea strictly on its own merits—as if he were unaware of its source? Where is the man who can say "yes" or "no" to friend or foe with equal detachment? So rare are such individuals that we run the risk of concluding that no such person exists.

However, we must not despair. Recently, I was presented with an idea by an unknown author—in these words: *"There is no such thing as a broken commitment."* Observing on many occasions that people do actually go back on their bond, I thought this to be at odds with the facts of life. Later, its meaning was explained to me: An unbroken commitment in this context means something more than paying debts, keeping promises, observing contracts. *A man has a commitment to his own conscience, that is, to truth as his highest conscience discerns truth, and every word and deed must be an accurate reflection thereof.* No pressure of fame or fortune or love or hate can even tempt such a person to compromise his integrity. At this level of life there can be no broken commitment.

Incorruptibility in its intellectual and spiritual sense refers to a higher order of men than is generally known to exist. It relates to men whose moral nature is such that infidelity to conscience is as unthinkable to them as stealing pennies from a child's bank is to us. Folks who would deviate from their own highest concept of righteousness simply are not of this order nor are they likely to be aware that there is such an order of men.

An interesting sidelight on the individual whose prime engagement is with his own conscience and who is not swerved by popular acclaim or the lack of it, is that he seldom knows who his incorruptible brothers are. They are, by their nature—all of them—a quiet lot; indeed, most of us are lucky if we ever spot one.

Signs of Corruption

At this moment in history, this order of men must be distressingly small. The reason for this opinion is the "respectability" which presently attends all but the basest forms of corruption. Almost no shame descends upon seekers after office who peddle pure hokum in exchange for votes; they sell their souls for political power and become the darlings of the very people on whom their wiles are practiced. Business and professional men and women, farmers and workers, through their associations and lobbies, clergymen from their pulpits, and teachers before their students shamelessly advocate special privileges: the feathering of the nests of some at the expense of others—and by coercion! For so doing they receive far more pious acclaim than censure. Such are the signs of widespread corruption.

As further evidence of intellectual corruption, reflect on the growing extent to which excuses are advanced as if they were reasons. In the politico-economic realm, for example, we put an embargo on goods from China because they are, in fact, competitive. But professing to favor free, competitive enterprise, and hesitating to confess that we are against competition, we corrupt ourselves and offer the excuse that these goods are "red."

Caviar from Russia—noncompetitive—is imported by the ton but is just as "red" as a linen tablecloth from

China. This type of corruption occurs on an enormous scale, but is shrugged off as "good business." Things would be otherwise if incorruptibility were more common.

If I am not mistaken, several rare, incorruptible oversouls have passed my way during these last three decades. For one thing, they were different. But it cannot be said that they stood out from the rest of us for, to borrow a phrase from a Chinese sage, they all operated in "creative quietness." While not standing out, they were outstanding—that is, their positions were always dictated by what they believed to be right. This was their integrity. They consistently, everlastingly sought for the right. This was their intelligence. Furthermore, their integrity and intelligence imparted to them a wisdom few ever attain: a sense of being men, not gods, and, as a consequence, an awareness of their inability to run the lives of others. This was their humility. Lastly, they never did to others that which they would not have others do to them. This was their justice.

Truth will out, with enough of these incorruptible souls!

The Truth About Freedom

Now, having staked out the ideal, it behooves me to approximate it as best I can, which is to say, to present the truth as I see it, in this instance, as it bears on the free market and related institutions.

By my title, "Anything That's Peaceful," I mean let anyone do anything he pleases that's peaceful or creative; let there be no organized restraint against anything but fraud, violence, misrepresentation, predation; let anyone deliver mail or educate or preach his religion or whatever, so long as it's peaceful; limit society's agency of organized force—government—to juridical and policing functions, tabulating the do-nots and prescribing the penalties against unpeaceful actions; let the government do this and leave all else to the free, unfettered market!

All of this, I concede, is an affront to the mores. So be it!

One more point: Discussion of ideological questions is more or less idle unless there be an awareness of what the major premise is. At what is the writer aiming? Is he doing his reasoning with some purpose in mind? If so, what is it?

I do not wish to leave anyone in the dark concerning my basic point of reference. Realizing years ago that I couldn't possibly be consistent in my positions unless I reasoned from a basic premise—fundamental point of reference—I set about it by asking one of the most difficult of questions: What is man's earthly purpose?

I could find no answer to that question without bumping, head on, into three of my basic assumptions. The first derives from the observation that man did not create himself, for there is evidence aplenty that man knows very little about himself, thus:

1. The primacy and supremacy of an Infinite Consciousness;
2. The expansibility of individual consciousness, this being demonstrably possible; and
3. The immortality of the individual spirit or consciousness, our earthly moments being not all there is to it—this being something I know but know not how to demonstrate.

With these assumptions, the answer to the question, "What is man's earthly purpose?" comes clear: *It is to ex-*

pand one's own consciousness into as near a harmony with Infinite Consciousness as is within the power of each, or, in more lay terms, to see how nearly one can come to a realization of those creative potentialities peculiar to one's own person, each of us being different in this respect.

This is my major premise with which the reader may or may not agree but he can, at least, decide for himself whether or not the following chapters are reasoned logically from this basic point of reference.

The ideas offered here have been brewing for several years. Many of them, though slightly rephrased, have appeared elsewhere as separate essays. My aim now is to gather those fragments into an integrated, free market theme.

CHAPTER 2

THE AMERICAN SETTING: PAST AND PRESENT

SOMEONE ONCE SAID: It isn't that Christianity has been tried and found wanting; it has been tried and found difficult—and abandoned. Perhaps the same running away from righteousness is responsible for freedom's plight for, plainly, the American people are becoming more and more afraid of and are running away from—abandoning—their very own freedom revolution.

Freedom, it seems to me, is of two broad types, psychological and sociological. The psychological—perhaps the more important of the two, but not the major concern of this book—has to do with man freeing himself from his own superstitions, myths, fears, imperfections, ignorance. This, of course, is a never-ending task to which we should give a high priority.

The sociological aspect of freedom, on the other hand, has to do with man imposing his will by force on other men. It is unfortunate that we need to spend any time on this part of the problem, for it calls for combating a situation that should not be. For instance, it is absurd for me forcibly to impose my will upon you: dictate what you are to discover, invent, create, where you shall work, the hours of your labor, the wage you shall receive, what and with whom you shall exchange. And it is just as absurd for any two or even millions or any agency that the millions may contrive—government or otherwise—to try to forcibly direct and control your creative or productive or peaceful actions.

Light can be shed on this thought by reflecting on the manner in which human energy manifests itself. Broadly speaking, it shows forth as either peaceful or unpeaceful, which is to say, as creative or destructive. If my hand is used to paint a picture, write this book, build a home, strew seed, my energy is manifestly peaceful, creative, productive. But if I make a clenched fist of the same hand and strike you with it, my energy is manifestly unpeaceful, destructive.

My theme is that any one of us has a moral right to inhibit the destructive actions of another or others, and, by the same token, we have a right to organize (government) to accomplish this universal right to life, livelihood, liberty. But no living person or any combination of persons, regardless of how organized, has a moral right forcibly to direct and control the peaceful, creative, productive actions of another or others. To repeat, we should not find it necessary to devote time and thought to this sociological aspect of the freedom problem, but a brief sketch of the American setting, past and present, will demonstrate that an awakening is now "a must" of the first order.

Let us pick up the thread of the historical setting beginning with the year 1620 when our Pilgrim Fathers landed at Plymouth Rock. That little colony began by practicing communism; all that was produced by each member, regardless of how much or how little, was forced (unpeaceful) into a common warehouse and the proceeds of the warehouse were doled out in accord with the governing body's idea of the need. In short, our Pilgrim Fathers began the practice of a principle that was advanced by Karl Marx—more than two centuries later—as the ideal of the Communist Party: "from each according to his ability, to each according to his need."

There was a persuasive reason why the Pilgrims threw overboard this communalistic or communistic practice: the members were starving and dying because, when people are organized in this manner, the warehouse always runs out of provender. The stark reality of the situation suggested to them that their theory was wrong and, bless them, they paused for reflection. In the third winter when they met with Governor Bradford, he said to them, in effect: Come spring, we'll try a new idea. We'll cast aside this communistic notion of to each according to need and try the idea of to each according to merit. Come spring, and each of you shall have what each produces.

As the record has it, springtime witnessed not only father in the field but mother and the children as well. Governor Bradford reported much later, "Any generall wante or famine hath not been amongst them since to this day."[1]

It was by reason of the practice of this private property principle that there began in this land of ours an era of

---

[1] Taken from *Bradford's History "of Plimoth Plantation"* from the original manuscript. Printed under the direction of the Secretary of the Commonwealth by order of the General Court (Boston: Wright & Potter Printing Company, State Printers, 1898), p. 162.

growth and development which sooner or later had to lead to revolutionary political ideas. And it did lead to what I refer to as the real American revolution, the revolution from which more and more Americans are now running away, as if in fear.

A Revolutionary Concept

The real American revolution, however, was not the armed conflict we had with King George III. That was a reasonably minor fracas as such fracases go! The real revolution was a novel concept or idea which was a break with all political history. It was something politically new on earth!

Until 1776 men had been contesting with each other—killing each other by the millions—over the age-old question of which of the numerous forms of authoritarianism —that is, man-made authorities—should preside as sovereign over man. The argument was not which was better, freedom or authoritarianism, but which of the several forms of authoritarianism was the least bad. And then, in 1776, in the fraction of one sentence written into the Declaration of Independence, was stated the real American revolution, the new idea, and it was this: "that all men . . . are endowed by their Creator with certain unalienable Rights; that among these are Life, Liberty and the pursuit of Happiness." There you have it! This is the essence of the original American setting and the rock on which the "American miracle" was founded.

The revolutionary idea was at once a spiritual, a political, and an economic concept. It was spiritual in that the writers of the Declaration recognized and publicly proclaimed that the Creator was the endower of man's rights; and, thus, it follows, that the Creator is sovereign.

It was political in that it implicitly denied that the state is the endower of man's rights, thus holding to the tenet that the state is not sovereign.

Our revolutionary concept was economic in this sense: that if an individual has a right to his life, it follows that he has a right to sustain his life—the sustenance of life being nothing more nor less than the fruits of one's labor.

It is one thing intellectually to embrace such a revolutionary concept as this; it is quite another matter to implement it—to put it into practice. The implementation came in the form of two political instruments—the Constitution and the Bill of Rights. These were essentially a series of prohibitions—prohibitions not against the people but against the political arrangement the people, from their Old World experience, had learned to fear, namely, over-extended government.[2]

The Constitution and the Bill of Rights more severely limited government than government had ever before been limited. There were benefits that flowed from this limitation of the state.

The first benefit, once this new concept became effective, was that individuals did not turn to government for security, welfare, or prosperity because government was so limited that it had little on hand to dispense; nor did its lim-

---

[2] The Constitution and the Bill of Rights specify 46 negations of governmental actions.

ited power permit taking from some citizens and giving to others. To what or to whom do people turn for security, welfare, and prosperity when government is not available to them? They turn to where they should turn—to themselves.

As a result of this discipline founded on the revolutionary concept that the Creator, not the state, is the endower of man's rights, along with these instruments of limitation, there was developed, on an unprecedented scale, a quality of character that Emerson referred to as "self-reliance." The American people gained a world-wide reputation for being self-reliant.

A second benefit that flowed from this severe limitation of government: When government is limited to inhibiting the destructive actions of men, when it sticks to its sole competency of keeping the peace and invoking a common justice, which is to say, when it minimizes such unpeaceful actions as fraud, violence, predation, misrepresentation —when it is thus limited—then there is no organized force standing against the peaceful, productive, creative actions of citizens. As a consequence of this limitation, there was a freeing, a releasing of creative energy, on a scale unheard of before.

I repeat, it was this combination which was chiefly responsible for the veritable outburst of creative human energy and that accounted for the "American miracle." We must everlastingly keep in mind that its roots were in the revolutionary concept that the Creator, not the state, is the endower of man's rights.

This keeping-the-peace design manifested itself in in-

dividual freedom of choice as related to all peaceful, productive, creative efforts. Citizens had freedom of choice
as to how they employed themselves; they had freedom
of choice as to how they priced their own labor or steel or
whatever; they had freedom of choice as to what they did
with their own income.

This is the American setting—*as it was.*

The Situation in America Today

But let us examine the American setting *as it is,* a reversal in form, one might say. It seems that the persons we
placed in government as our agents of peace discovered a
weakness in our unique structure. Having acquisitive instincts for power over others—as indeed so many of us do—
they found that the police power they had been given to
keep the peace could be used to invade the peaceful, productive, creative areas the citizens had reserved for themselves—one of which was the business sector. And they
also discovered that if they incurred any deficits by their
interventions, the same police force could be used to collect
the wherewithal to pay the bills. The very same force that
can be used to protect against predation can also be used
predatorily!

It is this misuse of police force, so little understood, which
explains why we Americans who inveigh vociferously against
socialism are unwittingly adopting socialism ourselves. For
it is clear that the extent to which government has departed
from the original design of inhibiting the unpeaceful and
destructive actions; the extent to which government has

invaded the peaceful, productive, creative areas; the extent to which our government has assumed the responsibility for the security, welfare, and prosperity of the citizenry is a measure of the extent to which socialism—communism, if you choose—has developed in this land of ours.

Can we measure this political devolution? Yes, with near precision. Reflect on one of the manifestations of the original structure: each individual having freedom of choice as to how he disposes of his own income. Measure the loss in this freedom of choice and you measure the gain of socialism. Merely bear in mind that freedom of choice exists except as restraint is interposed. Thus, the loss in freedom of choice shows the gain in authoritarian socialism.

The Growth of Government

Let us, then, proceed with the measurement. About 125 years ago the average citizen had somewhere between 95 and 98 per cent freedom of choice with each income dollar; which is to say, the tax take of government—federal, state, and local—was between 2 and 5 per cent of the people's earned income. But, as the emphasis shifted from the original design, as government invaded the peaceful, productive, and creative areas, and as government assumed more and more the responsibility for the security, welfare, and prosperity of the people, the percentage of the take of total earned income increased. The 2 to 5 per cent take of a relatively small income has steadily grown to a take of approximately 36 per cent of a very large earned income—and grows apace!

Many complacent persons, undaunted by this ominous trend, remark: "Why fret about this; we still have remaining to us, *on the average,* 64 per cent freedom of choice with respect to each income dollar.

Parenthetically, may I suggest that we use with care the term "on the average." Assume a 40-hour week, 8 hours a day, Monday through Friday. The *average* person, today, must work all of Monday and until mid-afternoon on Tuesday for government before he can begin to work for himself. But, if the individual has been extraordinarily successful, he has to work all of Monday, Tuesday, Wednesday, Thursday, and until noon on Friday for the government before he can start working for himself. He has only Friday afternoon to labor for his freedom-of-choice dollars. This, it seems, is a part of the "new" incentive system!

While we still enjoy 64 per cent freedom of choice over our earned income, this should afford little consolation. For we've long passed in this country the historical 20 to 25 per cent tax level beyond which governments seldom have gone without resorting to inflation. We are well into the inflationary stage, which means that constitutional or institutional limits on the taxing power have been abandoned; the government has found a way to take all our earned income if and when it chooses to do so.

Are we inflating? Indeed, yes! Let me explain that by "inflation" I do not mean rising prices, a consequence of inflation; rather, I mean government's expansion of the volume of money. To the economist or mathematician, inflation is the same as counterfeiting; to the lawyer, inflation is distinguished from counterfeiting by being legal. But, definitions aside, governments always have popular support for their inflationary policies; politicians act in response to popular support; they cannot remain in office without it. Why the popular support? It is because a majority of voters are naive enough to believe that they can eat their cake and still have their cake left to them, which is to say, they can continue to receive handouts and "benefits" from government without having to pay for them. Because they see no direct tax levy and because they do not understand that inflation is a cruel, unjust form of taxation, they applaud the something which they feel is coming to them for nothing.

Inflationary Devices

It is interesting to observe the tricks of inflation—political sleight-of-hand, coin clipping, for instance. The sovereign of old—by police force, that is, unpeacefully—"called in" the coin of the realm, clipped the edges, retained the clippings, and returned the balance to the owners. This skulduggery continued until the coins became too small to return.

The French Revolution put that government in dire financial straits, so it issued, in ever-larger amounts, an irredeemable paper money, known as *assignats,* secured not by gold but by confiscated church properties. Every American should read and know by heart the catastrophic aftermath.[3]

---

[3] See *Fiat Money Inflation in France* by Andrew Dickson White (Irvington-on-Hudson, N. Y.: Foundation for Economic Education, Inc., 1959).

In Argentina—following Perón and until recently—the
expense of the national government was, shall we say, 100
billion pesos annually. But only half that amount could be
collected by direct tax levies. How handled? Simple! They
merely printed 50 billion pesos annually. One need not be
much of an economist to realize that when the money
volume is expanded, everything else being equal, the value
of the monetary unit declines; prices rise. Imagine yourself
"secure" at the time of Perón's ascendancy to power: bank
accounts, insurance, social security, a pension for your old
age. These, along with all forms of fixed income, were politically rendered more or less worthless.

Our inflationary scheme in the U.S.A. is brilliant leger-
demain: it is so complex that hardly anyone can understand it! We monetize debt; that is, the more the government spends, the more is the money supply expanded. Since
the start of deficit financing and monetized debt, our quantity of dollars has enormously increased. Anyone with an
eye to trends can observe that the dollar has declined in
value and that prices are on the upswing.

The Russians, in my judgment, have the most honest
system of dishonesty: the Kremlin—with guns, if necessary
—"calls upon" the people to purchase government bonds.
After the people have bought the bonds, the government
cancels the bonds. Certainly, one does not have to be an
economist to observe the chicanery in this method of inflation.

Frankly, I wish we were employing the Russian system of
dishonesty rather than our present complex system. Were we
inflating in this crude Russian manner, many Americans

would be aware of what is being done to them. People who can't see through shell games are likely to be taken in.

This is what we must realize: Inflation is the fiscal concomitant of socialism or the welfare state or state interventionism—call these unpeaceful, political structures what you will. Politically, it isn't possible to finance government expenditures by direct tax levies beyond the point at which direct tax levies are politically expedient—20-25 per cent, as a rule. The overextended state is always beyond this point. Thus, anyone who does not like inflation can do nothing about it except as he assists in divesting our economy of socialism.

A good economy, in one respect, is analogous to a sponge; it can sop up a lot of mess. But once the sponge is saturated, the sponge itself is a mess. The only way to make it useful again is to wring the mess out of it.

Inflation in Modern France

Inflation may be better understood if we analyze it in some country other than our own; it is difficult to see our own faults, easy to note the mistakes of others. France serves our purpose, for that country, economically, has many likenesses to the U.S.A.

In 1914—only 50 years ago—modern France began what is now underway here; that is, her government invaded the peaceful, productive, creative areas and more and more assumed the responsibility for the security, welfare, and prosperity of the French people: socialism.

If my previous contentions be correct, the franc should

have lost some of its purchasing value during these 50 years. To repeat, I have contended that socialism can be financed only by inflation which is an expansion of money volume —with a consequent price rise as money value declines. If my reasoning is valid, the franc should have declined in purchasing value. Has it? Yes, more than 99½ per cent!

In Paris, during World War I, I bought a good dinner for 5 francs, the equivalent of a 1918 dollar. On my next visit to Paris—1947—I took a friend to luncheon, admittedly a better restaurant than I visited as a soldier boy. How much for the two luncheons? 3,400 francs! Two years later I took my wife to the same restaurant and had the same luncheons, because it is instructive to check prices. How much? 4,100 francs! On a recent visit, same restaurant, same luncheons—6,000 francs!

Visualize a French lad in his early teens, forethoughtful, looking to 1964 when he would reach retirement. He bought a paid-up annuity, one that would return him 1,000 francs per month beginning in 1964. In 1914, the year of purchase, he could have lived quite handsomely on this amount. Yet, in 1964, the thousand francs will buy no more than a skimpy, low-grade meal, pretty poor fare for a whole month! This fictional catastrophe, in no way exaggerated, was brought about by an inevitable inflation in the name of social security.

The validity of this line of reasoning is confirmed historically: Only 35 years ago the take of earned income by government in Russia was 29 per cent; in Germany, 22 per cent; in England, 21 per cent. Keep in mind that we are now at 36 per cent and that our government has the policy of increasing expenditures as it reduces taxes, assuring more inflation which, of course, increases the take.

The "Galloping" Stage

Inflation, in popular terms, is of two types: "creeping" and "galloping." Ours is often described as "creeping," a term that appears rather weak to describe a dollar that has lost between 52 and 63 per cent of its purchasing value since 1939—according to which index one uses.

"Galloping" inflation is the type that Germany experienced following World War I and France during her issuance of the *assignats*. China's money went "galloping" not too long ago, and the same can be said for the Latin American currencies right now.

I own one piece of Bolivia's currency—10,000 Bolivianos. In 1935 it had the purchasing power of 4,600 of our 1964 dollars. What now? Eighty cents! There is galloping inflation for you and brought about—they had no wars—by socialism. In every instance "galloping" inflation has been preceded by "creeping" inflation. Not too strangely, inflation creeps before it gallops; and anyone having a dread of inflation should be on the alert whenever it begins to creep.

Any rational person should dread inflation, more so in the U.S.A. than elsewhere, and for self-evident reasons: Americans have a more advanced division-of-labor society than has heretofore existed; we are more specialized and further removed from self-subsistence than peoples of other times and places. I, for instance, do not know how to build my home, raise my food, make my clothes; with respect to most of what I consume, I know next to nothing. Like all other Americans—even farmers, for they are mechanized—I have become dependent on the free, uninhibited exchange of our countless specializations. Try to visualize existing on that which you alone produce!

A necessity is anything on which we have become dependent. Free, peaceful, unfettered exchange is as necessary to present-day Americans as is air or water.

There is, however, a key fact to keep in mind: In a highly specialized economy it is not possible to effect these necessary exchanges by barter. The woman who inspects transistors makes no attempt to barter the service she renders for a pair of shoes; nor do you observe a car owner trying to barter a goose for a gallon of gas.

No, an advanced division-of-labor economy cannot be made to function by direct swaps of this for that. Such an economy has only one means to effect the necessary exchanges of its numerous specializations: an economic circulatory system, that is, *a medium of exchange*—money.

Thinning the Blood

This economic circulatory system can be likened, in one respect, to the circulatory system of the body, the blood stream. Among other functions, the blood stream effects numerous exchanges: it picks up oxygen and ingested food, carrying these life givers to some 30 trillion cells of the body, and, at these trillions of points, it picks up carbon dioxide and waste matters, returning these items for disposal. But let someone insert a hypodermic needle into a vein, thin the blood stream—destroy its integrity—and the victim can be referred to in the past tense.

Likewise, one can thin the economic circulatory system by inflating—assured by socialism—and bring on the same catastrophic results; exchange will be impossible with each of us wedded to our specialization but unable to exchange our own for the specializations of others. The integrity of the medium of exchange has to be presupposed to assume that a division-of-labor economy can function for any sustained period of time.

To illustrate: Following the 1918 Armistice, my squadron was sent to Coblenz in the Army of Occupation. The German inflation was under way. I knew no more about inflation then than do most of our citizens now. And like many people, I enjoyed what I experienced: more marks each pay day, but not because of any increase in salary. The government was taking care of my food, shelter, clothing— I had "security." My marks were used mostly to play games of chance—the more marks the more fun. Why shouldn't I enjoy inflation?

The German inflation continued with mounting intensity; by 1923 it reached a point where 30 million marks would not buy a loaf of bread.

About the time I arrived in Coblenz (this is fiction, but sound) an elderly German passed on, leaving his fortune to his two sons—500,000 marks each. One was a frugal lad; he never spent a pfennig of it. The other was a playboy; he spent the whole inheritance on champagne parties. When the day came in 1923 that 30 million marks wouldn't buy a loaf of bread, the lad who had saved everything, had nothing. But the other was able to exchange his empty champagne bottles for a dinner! The economy had been reduced to barter. To fully grasp the present American setting, we must be able to see that this very process is gaining momentum in our own economy. And primarily because we are substituting socialism for the peaceful ways of the free market.

At this point it is appropriate to be hardheaded and ask a practical question: Has there ever been an instance, historically, when a country has been on our kind of a socialistic toboggan and succeeded in reversing herself? There was a 10-year turnabout in the city-state of Lagash circa 2500 B.C., a 2-year reversal in the France of Turgot in the eighteenth century and, perhaps, there have been other minor cases of such political heroism. But, for the most part, the record reads like "the decline and fall of the Roman Empire."

The only significant turnabout known to me took place in England following the Napoleonic Wars. The nation's debt, in relation to her resources, must have been greater than ours now is; the taxation was confiscatory; and the restrictions on the peaceful production and exchange of goods and services—along with price controls—were so numerous and inhibitory that had it not been for the smugglers, black marketeers, and breakers of the law, many would have starved.[4] Altogether, a bleak economic picture, indeed! Here, assuredly, was a setting worse than ours yet is.

---

[4] When the law runs amuck, lawlessness often ensues.

Something happened, unique in history; and it is well that we take cognizance of it. One thing for certain, the change was wrought by a handful of men. We have a good account of the work of Richard Cobden and John Bright in England and of their two French collaborators, a politician named Chevalier, and the political economist and essayist, Frederic Bastiat. Cobden and Bright, having a far better understanding of freedom-in-exchange principles than their contemporaries, went about England speaking and writing on the freedom philosophy. The economy was out of kilter; Members of Parliament listened and, as a consequence, there began the greatest reform movement in English history.

The reform consisted of the repeal of restrictive law; the peaceful ways of the market were made possible by the removal of unpeaceful governmental interventionism. The Corn Laws (tariffs) were repealed outright; the Poor Laws (relief) were greatly curtailed; there were numerous other repeals. And, fortunately for the people, their newly limited government, nominally headed by Queen Victoria, relaxed the authority which the people themselves believed to be implicit in their Sovereign; the government gave the people freedom in the sense that a prisoner on parole is free: he can be yanked back! But the government exercised no such control; Englishmen by the hundreds of thousands roamed over the face of the earth achieving unparalleled prosperity and building a relatively enlightened empire.

This development continued until just before World War I when the same old political disease set in again. What precisely is this disease that must result in inflation and other unpeaceful manifestations? It has many popular names, some already mentioned, such as socialism, communism, the welfare state, government interventionism, authoritarianism. It has other names such as fascism, nazism, Fabianism, the planned economy. It has local names like New Deal, Fair Deal, New Republicanism, New Frontier; and new ones will be contrived to suggest that the identical political arrangement has something novel about it.

Faith in Government Intervention

However, popular names are but generalizations and oversimplifications. What, then, is really the essence of the above-mentioned "progressive ideologies"? Careful scrutiny of their *avowed* aims will reveal that each has a characteristic common to the others, this characteristic being the cell in the body politic that has the capacity for inordinate growth and from which stems our countless unpeaceful troubles. It is in the form of a belief—a rapidly growing belief—in the use of organized police force (government) not with the emphasis on keeping the peace but on a political manipulation of the peaceful, productive, creative activities of the citizenry. An increased intervention in all markets—commodities, exchange, finance, education, housing, or whatever—is what the proponents of this multi-named system set forth as their promise. I am only repeating the claim they present with pride; check it out for yourself.

To illustrate: I can remember the time when, if a house were wanted, the customer would look to the free market to supply it. The first step involved someone wanting a house in preference to other alternatives; the initiative rested with the desiring consumer. Next, the reliance was on those who wished to compete in the building. Last, we relied on people who thought they saw some advantage to themselves in loaning the money for the tools, labor, and material. With our reliance on the peaceful procedures of the market, we built more square feet of housing per person than was ever built in any other country at any other time.

Yet, despite this remarkable accomplishment, more and more people are coming to believe that the free market should be shelved and that, in its stead, government should use its police force to take the income of some and give it, in the form of housing, to the government's idea of the needy. In other words, we are now practicing the principle used by the Pilgrim Fathers in 1620-23, and proclaimed as an ideal by Karl Marx in 1848: "from each according to his abilities, to each according to his needs," and by the use of organized police force! (Keep in mind that I have used housing only as an example; the same policy is being extended to all segments of the economy.)

Here is a crucial, important, and self-evident fact: With increasing belief in police force as a means to productive ends, the belief in men acting freely, competitively, co-operatively, privately, voluntarily must correspondingly diminish. As a reliance on political authoritarianism advances, a faith in free men suffers erosion and, finally, obliteration.

It would seem to follow that there is no remedy for our current devolution except as a faith in free men be restored. The evolution of such a faith, I suspect, will rest as much on an unbelief in authoritarianism as on a belief of what can be wrought by voluntarism. I propose to share and explain my unqualified skepticism of political rigging as well as my faith in the creativity and miraculous performances of free men in an unfettered, peaceful market.

So much for the American setting—past and present!

CHAPTER 3

STRIFE AS A WAY
OF LIFE

BROADLY SPEAKING, there are two opposing philosophies of human relationships. One commends that these relationships be in terms of peace and harmony. The other, while never overtly commended, operates by way of strife and violence. One is peaceful; the other unpeaceful.

When peace and harmony are adhered to, only willing exchange exists in the market place—the economics of reciprocity and practice of the Golden Rule. No special privilege is countenanced. All men are equal before the law, as before God. The life and the livelihood of a minority of one enjoys the same respect as the lives and livelihoods of majorities, for such rights are, as set forth in the Declaration of Independence, conceived to be an endowment of the Creator. Everyone is completely free to act creatively as his abilities and ambitions permit; no restraint in this respect—none whatsoever.

Abandon the ideal of peace and harmony and the only alternative is to embrace strife and violence, expressed ultimately as robbery and murder. Plunder, spoliation,

special privilege, feathering one's own nest at the expense
of others, doing one's own brand of good with the fruits
of the labor of others—coercive, destructive, and unpeaceful schemes of all sorts—fall within the order of strife
and violence.

Are we abandoning the ideal of peace and harmony and
drifting into the practice of strife and violence as a way of
life? That's the question to be examined in this chapter
—and answered in the affirmative.

At the outset, it is well to ask why so few people are
seriously concerned about this trend. William James may
have suggested the reason: "Now, there is a striking law
over which few people seem to have pondered. It is this:
That among all the differences which exist, the only ones
that interest us strongly are those *we do not take for
granted.*"[1]

Socialistic practices are now so ingrained in our thinking, so customary, so much a part of our mores, that we
take them for granted. No longer do we ponder them; no
longer do we even suspect that they are founded on strife
and violence. Once a socialistic practice has been Ameri-
canized it becomes a member of the family so to speak and,
as a consequence, is rarely suspected of any violent or evil
taint. With so much socialism now taken for granted, we
are inclined to think that only other countries condone and
practice strife and violence—not us.

Who, for instance, ever thinks of TVA as founded on
strife and violence? Or social security, federal urban re-

---

[1] See *The Will to Believe and Other Essays on Popular Philosophy*
(New York: Dover Publications, Inc., 1956), p. 257.

newal, public housing, foreign aid, farm and all other subsidies, the Post Office, rent control, other wage and price controls, all space projects other than for strictly defensive purposes, compulsory unionism, production controls, tariffs, and all other governmental protections against competition? Who ponders the fact that every one of these aspects of state socialism is an exemplification of strife and violence and that such practices are multiplying rapidly?

The word "violence," as here used, refers to a particular kind of force. Customarily, the word is applied indiscriminately to two distinct kinds of force, each as different from the other as an olive branch differs from a gun. One is defensive or repellent force. The other is initiated or aggressive force. If someone were to initiate such an action as flying at you with a dagger, that would be an example of aggressive force. It is this kind of force I call strife or violence. The force you would employ to repel the violence I would call defensive force.

Try to think of a single instance where aggressive force —strife or violence—is *morally* warranted. There is none. Violence is morally insupportable!

Defensive force is never an initial action. It comes into play only secondarily, that is, as the antidote to aggressive force or violence. Any individual has a moral right to defend his life, the fruits of his labor (that which sustains his life), and his liberty—by demeanor, by persuasion, or with a club if necessary. Defensive force *is* morally warranted.

Moral rights are exclusively the attributes of individuals. They inhere in no collective, governmental or otherwise. Thus, political officialdom, in sound theory, can have no rights of action which do not pre-exist as rights in the individuals who organize government. To argue contrarily is to construct a theory no more tenable than the Divine Right of Kings. For, if the right to government action does not originate with the organizers of said government, from whence does it come?

As the individual has the moral right to defend his life and property—a right common to all individuals, a universal right—he is within his rights to delegate this right of defense to a societal organization. We have here the logical prescription for government's limitation. It performs morally when it carries out the individual moral right of defense.

As the individual has no moral right to use aggressive force against another or others—a moral limitation common to all individuals—it follows that he cannot delegate that which he does not possess. Thus, his societal organization—government—has no moral right to aggress against another or others. To do so would be to employ strife or violence.

To repeat a point in the previous chapter, it is necessary to recognize that man's energies manifest themselves either destructively or creatively, peacefully or violently. It is the function of government to inhibit and to penalize the destructive or violent manifestations of human energy. It is a malfunction to inhibit, to penalize, to interfere in any way whatsoever with the peaceful or creative or productive manifestations of human energy. To do so is clearly to aggress, that is, to take violent action.

TVA Analyzed

In the light of these definitions, let us then consider the nature and impact of TVA or any of the other socialistic projects earlier mentioned. We may assume that you are living peaceably off the fruits of your own labor, including anything which you have acquired from others in willing exchange. You are aggressing against no one; therefore, there is no occasion for anyone's use of defensive force against you, defense being a secondary action against an initiated aggressive action. And, certainly, there is no moral sanction for anyone or any organization to take aggressive action against you.

Now, let us suppose that some people decide they want their power and light at a price lower than the market rate. To accomplish their purpose, they forcibly (with weapons, if necessary) collect the fruits of your peaceable labor in the form of capital to construct the power plant. Then they annually use force to take your income to defray the deficits of their operation—deficits incurred by reason of the sub-market rates they charge themselves for the power and light they use. The questions I wish to pose are these: Is any set of persons, regardless of how economically strapped they may be, morally warranted in any such action? Would not their project be founded on strife or violence? The answers to these questions are inescapably clear: such persons are thieves and criminals.

Very well. Move on to TVA. What distinguishes TVA from the above? Not a thing, except that in the case of TVA the immoral, aggressive, violent action has been legalized. This merely means that the law has been perverted so as to exonerate the "beneficiaries" from the customary penalties for criminal action. But the fact remains that TVA, and all other instances of state socialism, are founded on strife and violence!

Most people are inclined to scoff at this idea simply because they have never witnessed any instance of actual violence associated with TVA. They are blinded to what really takes place by the common acquiescence to socialistic measures, once these forms of Robin Hoodism are legalized. Everybody goes along. But wait!

Should not any conscionable citizen pause for reflection when he awakens to the fact that the people of his country are abandoning the ideal of peace and harmony and drifting into the practice of strife and violence as a way of life? The fact that this catastrophic change is taking place without many persons being aware of it is all the more reason to sound the alarm.

Founded on Violence

It is easy to demonstrate that all state socialism, of which TVA is but an instance, is founded on violence. Take the government's program of paying farmers not to grow tobacco, for example. Let us say that your share of the burden of this socialistic hocus-pocus is $50. Should you *absolutely* refuse to pay it, assuming you had $50 in assets, you would be killed—legally, of course—here in the U.S.A. in the year of Our Lord, 1964! If that isn't resting the subsidy program on violence, then, pray tell, what is violence?

Here's how to get yourself killed: When you get your bill from the Internal Revenue Service, remit the amount minus $50 with these words of explanation:

"I do not believe that citizens should be compelled to pay farmers for not growing tobacco. I do not believe in the farm subsidy program. My share of the cost of the whole program is $50, which I have deducted. Do not try to collect for I ABSOLUTELY refuse to pay for same."

The IRS will quickly inform you that this is a matter in which freedom of choice does not exist and will demand that you remit the $50.

You respond by merely referring the IRS to your original letter, calling attention to your use of the word *"absolutely."*

When the IRS becomes convinced that you mean business, your case will be referred to another branch of the government, the judicial apparatus. It being the function of the judiciary only to interpret the law, the law making it plain that a government claim has first lien on one's assets, a decision will be rendered against you and in favor of the IRS. If you have no assets but your home, the Court will order it put on the auction block and will instruct you to vacate.

At this point you will apprise the Court of your letter to the IRS and your use of the word *"absolutely."*

When the Court becomes convinced that you mean business, your case will be referred to still another branch of the government, the constabulary. In due course, a couple of officers carrying arms will attempt to carry out the Court's instructions. They will confront you in person.

But to accede to their "invitation" to vacate would be to
pay. With your *"absolutely"* in mind, you refuse. At this
point the officers in their attempt to carry out the Court's
orders will try to carry you off your property, as peaceably
as possible, of course. But to let them carry you off would
be to acquiesce and to pay. You might as well have acquiesced in the first place. At this stage of the proceed-
ings, in order not to pay, you have no recourse but to re-
sist physical force with physical force. It is reasonable to
assume that from this point on you will be mentioned only
in the past tense or as "the late Mr. You." The records will
show that your demise was "for resisting an officer," but
the real reason was that you *absolutely* refused to pay farmers for not growing tobacco or whatever.

Rarely will any citizen go this far. Most of us, regardless
of our beliefs, acquiesce immediately on receipt of the bill
from the IRS. But the reason we do so is our recognition
of the fact that this is an area in which freedom of choice
no longer exists. I, for instance, would never give a cent of
my income to farmers not to grow tobacco were I allowed
freedom of choice in the matter. But, realizing that the
farm subsidy program rests on violence, it takes no more
than the threat of violence to make me turn part of my
income over to farmers for not growing tobacco.

The Case of Mr. Byler

This idea that the whole wearisome list of socialistic
practices rests on strife and violence and that the ultimate
penalty for noncompliance is death, was written and pub-

lished in 1950.[2] Many have read the booklet and an explanation of the same idea has been given before many discussion groups throughout the country, but the reasoning has never been challenged. Yet, I am unaware of any instance where an individual has gone all the way, that is, has *absolutely* refused to pay and gone to his death for his beliefs. One farmer went so far as to leave the country, and quite a number of citizens have delayed their acquiescence considerably, that is, they have carried their revolt beyond immediate payment—usually mixed with grousing. One of the most interesting and instructive examples is reported by the IRS in a news release dated May 15, 1961:

> Considerable public and press misunderstanding exists over the seizure of three horses from a Pittsburgh area Amish farmer who refused to pay Social Security taxes because of religious convictions.
>
> This memo is designed merely to acquaint you with all the facts in the case.
>
> Public Law 761, 83rd Congress, effective January 1, 1955, extended Social Security coverage so as to include farm operators. A tax on the self-employment income of these people is imposed and they are required to report this tax on their annual federal income tax return.
>
> The Old Order Amish are the most conservative of the Amish groups and have taken the position that although they will comply with taxes, as such, Social Security payments, in their opinion, are insurance premiums and not taxes. They, therefore, will not pay the "premium" nor accept any of the benefits.
>
> In the fall of 1956, the IRS district director at Cleveland

---

[2] See my *Students of Liberty* (Irvington-on-Hudson, N. Y.: Foundation for Economic Education, Inc., 1950), pp. 7-8.

held meetings with Amish farmers and their church officials in an effort to solicit cooperation and voluntary compliance with the laws we have to administer. At these meetings, it was explained that the self-employment levy is a tax and that it would be the responsibility of IRS to enforce this tax.

As a result of these meetings and of letters sent to the individuals involved, the majority of Amish farmers in that general area voluntarily remitted the tax. With respect to those who refused, it became apparent that some did not wish to contravene the dictates of their church, but they also did not want "trouble" with IRS.

Thus, a portion of these farmers did not pay the tax, but did make the execution of liens possible by maintaining bank accounts which covered the tax.

The current problem stems from the "hard core" group of Old Order Amish farmers who closed out their bank accounts and made such levy action impossible. As a result, the IRS was forced to collect 130 delinquent taxpayer accounts from Amish farmers in the past two years.

Valentine Y. Byler of New Wilmington, Pennsylvania became the latest collection problem among the Old Order Amish. He owed the following self-employment tax:

1956	$82.60
1957	76.57
1958	32.98
1959	65.63

The foregoing taxes amounted to $257.78. The total interest for the same period was $51.18, making a grand total of $308.96 owed by the taxpayer.

Attempts had been made since 1956 to induce Mr. Byler to pay his tax willingly, but with no success. Since Mr. Byler had no bank account against which to levy for the tax due, it was decided as a last desperate measure to resort to seizure and sale of personal property.

It then was determined that Mr. Byler had a total of six horses, so it was decided to seize three in order to satisfy the tax indebtedness. The three horses were sold May 1, 1961, at public auction for $460. Of this amount $308.96 represented the tax due, and $113.15 represented expenses of the auction sale including feed for the horses, leaving a surplus of $37.80 which was returned to the taxpayer.

The Byler case like all others in the same category presents an unpleasant and difficult task for the Internal Revenue Service. However, there is no authority under which Amish farmers may be relieved of liability for this tax.

With respect to those who remain adamant in their refusal to pay, as in the case of any person who refuses to pay any federal tax that is lawfully due, it is incumbent on the Internal Revenue Service to proceed with collection enforcement action as provided by law.

We have no other choice under the law.

Had our Amish friend, Valentine Y. Byler, not acquiesced at the point he did but had gone all the way in his determination, he would have employed physical force against the officers who seized his three horses. In this event he would now be known as "the late Valentine Y. Byler." He would have established beyond a shadow of doubt that the Social Security program, as well as all other socialistic practices, is founded on strife and violence. These cannot, by any stretch of the imagination, come under the category of "peaceful actions."

Government Did Its Duty

It is important to acknowledge at this point that the IRS did precisely what it should have done. This agency of government is not in the business of deciding the rightness or wrongness of a tax. Its job is to collect regardless of what the tax is for.

The judiciary, having previously ruled on the powers of the IRS to make such collections, accurately interpreted the law and, thus, did what it should have done.

The constabulary, in seizing the three horses, was properly performing its function. This agency, unless derelict in its duty, has to look as indifferently on seizing the horses and harnesses of a gentle, God-fearing farmer as bringing a John Dillinger to bay. They are properly called *law enforcement* officers. And, had Mr. Byler resisted with physical force, the constabulary would have been performing its duty had it been found necessary to put Mr. Byler out of the way—as it did Dillinger. *Theirs is to carry out the law, not to reason why!*

The fault here is with the law, the three above-mentioned agencies being but effectuating arms of the law. And the fault with the law rests with those who make the law and with those of us who elect lawmakers and who, presumably, have some powers to reason *what* the law should be.

The IRS, the judiciary, the constabulary, behave exactly the same when seizing the Amish farmer's three horses as when collecting a fine for embezzlement. Yet, the former is an exercise of aggressive force—violence—while the latter is an exercise of defensive force. The former has no moral sanction; the latter is morally warranted. How can two police actions which ultimately manifest themselves in an identical manner actually be opposites? This is like asking how two shots from a pistol can be identical when one is used to protect life and property and the other is used to take life and property. The shots are wholly indifferent as to how they are used. The pistol shots, like the IRS, the judiciary, the constabulary, only do the bidding of someone's mind and will. It is the bidding which determines whether they are part of a defensive or an aggressive action. The law, and the people who are responsible for it, determine whether a police action is defensive or violent, whether it keeps the peace or acts unpeaceably.

There is, however, a simple way to decide whether a governmental action is an exercise of defensive force or an exercise of aggressive or violent force: "See if the law takes from some persons what belongs to them, and gives it to other persons to whom it does not belong. See if the law benefits one citizen at the expense of another by doing what the citizen himself cannot do without committing a crime."[3]

Using the above as a basis for determination, it is obvious that every act of state socialism is founded on violence. There are no exceptions.

"But We Didn't Mean This"

The fact that the IRS found it expedient to make a public explanation in the face of severe criticism throughout the country, merely lends credence to the fact that most people—even those who support socialistic legislation —do not know what they are doing nor did they mean to do what they did. Simply because most of us meekly acquiesce, that is, uncomplainingly go along with the machin-

---

[3] See *The Law* by Frederic Bastiat (Irvington-on-Hudson, N. Y., Foundation for Economic Education, Inc., 1950), 76 pp.

ery of socialism, we tend to lose sight of the fact that it is founded on strife and violence. The seizing of the Amish farmer's horses generated widespread feelings of remorse and resentment. Had he *absolutely* refused to pay and been killed in the process, the American people would have protested, *"But we didn't mean this!"*

Of course they didn't mean it. Nonetheless, these projections of property-seizure and even death are nothing more nor less than the inevitable consequences of admitting the socialistic premise into American policy. We need, now and then, to check our premises.

Alexander Barmine and Victor Kravchenko, both of whom rose to top posts in the Kremlin hierarchy, escaped from Russia and came to this country because they could not stomach the purgings and shootings that logically followed the policies which they themselves had a hand in promoting.[4] Let the principle of violence continue in this country—even fail to rid ourselves of what we already have—and gangsters only will come to occupy high political office. Few of the present crop of bureaucrats are heartless enough to administer socialism in its advanced stages.[5] Violence is not their dish. The IRS folks demonstrate this.

That policies founded on strife and violence are growing is evident enough to anyone who will take the pains

[4] See *One Who Survived* by Alexander Barmine (New York: G. A. Putnam's Sons), and *I Chose Freedom* by Victor Kravchenko (New York: Scribners, 1946).

[5] To understand why gangsters rather than humane human beings must occupy political office in a socialistic state, read "Why the Worst Get on Top" in F. A. Hayek's *The Road to Serfdom* (Chicago: University of Chicago Press, 1944). Obtainable from the Foundation for Economic Education, Inc., Irvington-on-Hudson, N. Y.

to look. Reflect on the examples of practices founded on violence cited earlier in this chapter. All but the Post Office are of relatively recent vintage, with increasing clamor for more of the same.

I can still remember when the income of farmers came from willing exchange; when people lived in houses built with the fruits of their own labor; when wage earners, for the most part, were no more compelled to join unions than businessmen are now forced into chamber of commerce membership or parents into the P.T.A. In those days, "peaceful" far better described the way of life than did strife and violence.

Man either accepts the idea that the Creator is the endower of rights, or he submits to the idea that the state is the endower of rights. I can think of no other alternative.

Those who accept the Creator concept can never subscribe to the practice of violence in any form. They have been drawn to this concept, not coerced into it. If we would emulate, as nearly as we can, that which we have learned from this relationship, we would confine ourselves to this same drawing power. As Gerald Heard so clearly puts it, "Man is free to torture himself until he sees that his methods are not those of his Maker."[6]

---

[6] Gerald Heard, editor, *Prayers and Meditations* (New York: Harper & Brothers, 1949), p. 39.

CHAPTER 4

SOCIALISM
IS NONCREATIVE

Socialism depends upon and presupposes material achievements which socialism itself can never create. Socialism is operative only in wealth situations brought about by modes of production other than its own. Socialism takes and redistributes wealth, but it is utterly incapable of creating wealth.[1]

Few Americans today would object were this devastating indictment leveled against communism. But to accuse the U.S.A. brand of democratic socialism of barrenness or sterility is to put the shoe on another foot. Are you actually implying, many will ask, that a vast majority of Americans are rapidly committing themselves to a will-o'-the-wisp? Eating the seed corn? Sponsoring parasitism? Yes, this is the charge, and I shall do my best to demonstrate its truth.

Socializing the *means* of production and socializing the

---

[1] This chapter refers only to the creative sterility of socialism, its unproductivity. But even if socialism were the most productive of all economic systems, it would not meet with my approval. Socialism de-emphasizes self-responsibility and, thus, is contrary to my major premise which is founded on the emergence of the individual.

results of production are but two sides of the same coin, inseparable in practice. The state that controls production is going to control the distribution of what is produced; and the state that distributes the product must, eventually, control production.

That inescapable fact is just as true in the United States, with its democratic socialism, as it is in Russia with its dictatorial socialism. In our own country, when we refer to the "planned economy," we mean that wages, hours, prices, production, and exchange shall be largely determined by state directives—and not by free response to market decisions. Though our "welfare state" policies are currently more humane than their counterparts in Russia, socialism in both nations, whether having to do with the *means* or the *results* of production, rests on organized police force.

Socialism is more than a some-other-country folly. It demands a hard look at what our own American mirror reveals. My purpose is self-analysis, not a discourse on the political antics of power-drunk Russians.

Now to return to my opening assumption: *Socialism depends upon and presupposes material achievements which socialism itself can never create.*

This indictment has two parts: (1) there has to be wealth before wealth can be socialized; and (2) socialism cannot create the wealth in the first place.

With everyone's wealth at zero, there is no one from whom anything can be taken. Many of our Pilgrim Fathers starved during the first three years of community communism because there was so little in the warehouse to

dole out. Communism—or one of our numerous names
for the same thing, the welfare state—presupposes the existence of wealth which can be forcibly extorted. Is this not
self-evident?

There remains, then, only to show that socialism—the
planned economy side of the coin—cannot give rise to the
means of production; that is, state ownership and control
of the means of production cannot create the wealth on
which state welfarism rests.

The Pilgrims' warehouse was empty because the communistic mode of production couldn't fill it. The standard
of living of the Russian people is so much lower today
than our own because their avowed but not wholly practiced system is productively sterile.[2] Such goods as the Pilgrims did produce during their first three years, or as the
Russians now produce, can be explained only as the result
of deviations from socialism: *leakages of free, creative
human energies!* Had the Pilgrims practiced socialism 100
per cent, all the Pilgrims would have perished. Were the
Russians practicing socialism 100 per cent, there would
not be a living Russian. Life goes on in these and all other

---

[2] While state planning of the economy, and the coercive implementation of the state's plans are more widely practiced in Russia than perhaps any other country except China, we must remember that the
Kremlin is more and more disregarding its own tenets and edging
gradually toward the practice of a market economy. Incentives to induce production are on the increase, and a significant acreage has been
restored to a free market type of farming. What a picture: Russians
damning capitalism as they drift into capitalistic practices, and Americans damning communism as they drift into communistic ways of life!
Russians are so impoverished that they must turn to capitalistic reali-
ties; Americans are so affluent that they indulge themselves, at their
peril, in communistic nonsense.

socialistically-inclined societies because their inhabitants do not practice the socialistic theory totally! If I can demonstrate this point, my original indictment becomes unassailable.

Plato's Definition of Socialism

What actually is meant by total socialism? As a hint, here is a statement by Plato:

> The greatest principle of all is that nobody, whether male or female, should be without a leader. Nor should the mind of anybody be habituated to letting him do anything at all on his own initiative; neither out of zeal, nor even playfully. But in war and in the midst of peace—to his leader he shall direct his eye and follow him faithfully. And even in the smallest matter he should stand under leadership. For example, he should get up, or move, or wash, or take his meals . . . only if he has been told to do so. In a word, he should teach his soul, by long habit, never to dream of acting independently, and to become utterly incapable of it.[3]

The above quotation, however, does not describe socialism. It only outlines the extent to which an individual might become a selfless nonentity, *willingly* subserving a leader, dog fashion. If socialism were total, this recommended subservience would be brought about not by voluntary adoption but involuntarily, and by a master's coercion. In short, *total socialism means the total elimination of all volitional actions;* it means people in the role of robots. Freedom of choice on any matter would be nonexistent. Coercion is of its essence.

---

[3] Karl R. Popper. *The Open Society and Its Enemies* (Princeton: Princeton University Press, 1950), p. 9.

Now, consider the nature of coercive force. What can it do and what are its limitations? This is to ask what can be done by and what are the limitations of a gun, a billy club, a clenched fist. Clearly, they can inhibit, restrain, penalize, destroy. These are the identical possibilities and limitations of law or decree backed by force. Nothing more! *Law and decree cannot serve as a creative force,* any more than can a gun.

Coercively directed action can create nothing. Consider the driving of an automobile. No person would be a safe driver if he had to think his way through each act of steering, accelerating, or braking. Add the time it takes for numerous decisions to travel from the brain to the hands and feet, and it becomes plain that if drivers operated this way, one wreck would follow another. Any person who knows how to drive has succeeded in relegating driving's countless motions to the control of something akin to the autonomic nervous system. To know requires that one's responses become as automatic as breathing or writing; that is, become conditioned reflexes.

Now, consider a situation in which the relationship between decision and action is greatly complicated: a gunman in the back seat employing *his* thinking to command even the minutest actions of the driver. There could be no driving at all!

No driving at all? None whatsoever! Try an experiment: A coat hangs over the back of a chair. Find a person intelligent enough to dismiss absolutely all his knowledge of a coat, and capable of refraining from any and all volitional action, one who can force himself to be utterly incapable of independent, volitional response. In this situation, instruct him how to don the coat. He'll never get it on.

The above explanations and assertions, however, have to do only with the first essential of creative action, that is, volitional action. That coercion cannot induce even this is a fact that appears to be self-evident.

Production in Spite of Controls

Socialism, we must admit, gives the illusion of being productive. The productivity, however, exists in spite of socialism, not because of it. The productivity originates in the free, creative energy which ignores or escapes socialism's repression; that is, which oozes through or around socialism's smothering blanket. In England, following the Napoleonic Wars, and in the U.S.A. under the NRA and OPA, legal restrictions blanketed large areas of production and exchange. But note this: neither country's socialistic decrees were entirely obeyed. In each instance there were gross violations of socialism, with the result that the people managed to live. Such material well-being as there was appeared to come from socialism. It actually came, however, from free, creative energy which, for obvious reasons, was more or less unpublicized.

Numerous other distractions help to hide socialism's essential sterility. For instance, we observe that many government schoolteachers act no less creatively than do teachers of private schools. Scientists in the employ of government have inventive experiences, as do independent scientists and those in corporate employ. TVA, a socialistic enterprise, produces electrical energy of the same quality as that from an investor-owned plant. Agents of the state and private citizens more or less look alike, dress alike, behave alike. We choose our friends as often from one set as from the other. Meeting a stranger, one could not tell from appearance only to which category he belongs.

If we would properly evaluate the effect of coercion, with its total absence of creativeness, we should have to disregard these distractions. We need to recognize that it is not the government schoolteacher who exercises the three types of coercion implicit in socialistic education: (1) compulsory attendance, (2) government dictated curricula, and (3) the forcible collection of the wherewithal to pay the bills. Furthermore, we rarely feel any coercions simply because we meekly obey the laws backed by force; that is, we *do* send our children to school, we *do not* prescribe our own curricula, we *do* pay the tax bill. But refuse to acquiesce in any one of these three phases of compulsion and see what happens!

The scientist employed by the state, trying to figure out how to put three men on the moon, exercises no coercion. The coercion is applied to the collection of the funds which pay him to work as a free agent. He will work just as freely, as creatively, regardless of how his salary is collected. A billion dollars, whether garnered at the point of a gun or voluntarily donated, is in either case a billion dollars. A dollar extorted or a dollar freely given is still a dollar, with a dollar's purchasing power.

In the absence of socialism's coercion, each dollar would be used in accord with its owner's choice, to buy food or clothing, to educate the children, to take a vacation, to buy a sailboat. Coercion only diverts the dollars from owner use and puts them to state use. If, as predicted, putting three men on the moon will cost $20 billion to $40 billion, then that much freedom of choice will be destroyed. This enormous portion of our productivity will be socialized. The people are coercively relieved of their individual choices in order to permit a single choice, exercised by whoever heads the socialistic regime. Authoritarianism is forcibly substituted for individual liberty. What we witness here is a diversionary process accomplished by police action.

We will go astray in our analysis of this complex process unless we examine coercion at one of its points of impact —for instance, the impact on the citizens who are forced to foot the bills. So, ask yourself this question: Is the extortion of your income (in order that another may have the say-so as to what it will be spent for) a creative act? Does it make any difference to what use the other will put it? Charity, relief, moon shots, or whatever? Does it make any real difference whether or not the other is a person or a collective? There is no rational, affirmative answer to these questions. Extortion—coercion—is destructive. *It destroys your freedom of choice!* Coercion, by its nature, is destructive.

Let's draw an illustrative distinction between the coercive act and the creative act. A slap in the face (or the threat thereof) is a mild example of coercion. It is milder than the penalty for *absolutely* refusing to pay one's tax for a federal urban renewal project in somebody else's town.

structive force ever devised by man? But putting aside the
H-bomb, and such miraculous and fascinating follies as
orbiting monkeys and men around our earth, reflect on
the countless economy-destroying projects that result from
man lording it over his fellow men. Man cannot feign the
role of God without finally playing the devil's part. This
is to say, as Emerson so eloquently phrased it:

> Cause and effect, means and ends, seed and fruit, cannot be
> severed; for the effect already blooms in the cause, the end
> pre-exists in the means, the fruit in the seed.[6]

Stated in other terms, man cannot use coercion for other
than destructive purposes; for even a legitimate police action
for defense is still an inhibiting or destructive action, however necessary a police force may be. Raise billions by de-
stroying freedom of choice—the socialist format—and the
creative energies the funds finance will rarely serve the
higher ends of life. Three men on the moon, farmers paid
not to farm, flood control that floods land forever, mail
delivery that bears a $3 million daily deficit, the rebuild-
ing of urban areas that the market has deserted, the financing of socialistic governments the world over, are cases in
point. None of these is a creative or productive endeavor
in the full sense of those terms.

I began this chapter with the resolve to demonstrate that
socialism depends upon and presupposes material achievements which socialism itself cannot create, that socialism
is productively sterile. But after thinking it through, I

---

[6] From *The Complete Essays and Other Writings of Ralph Waldo
Emerson* (New York, N. Y.: The Modern Library, 1940), p. 176.

must confess that my affirmation can be proven only to those persons who see the long-range effects of present actions; and to those who *know* that man playing God is a prime evil, an evil seed that must grow to a destructive bloom, however pretty it may appear in its earlier stages.

At the outset, we must not assume common agreement that harm is visited only on the person from whom is taken. There are many well-to-do individuals, sensitive to the plight or suffering of others, who gladly turn over to government the responsibility of caring for all afflicted people and, along with this shifting of responsibility from themselves to the state, a willingness for the government to draw on (tax) their ability to pay. They, not I, should be the judge of the harm such shifting of responsibility does to them. I can only question their judgment.

Division of labor—me to my speciality, you to yours—is essential to an expanding wealth. But there are several aspects of life we cannot turn over to others without harm to our individual expansion. Religion cannot be shifted to others, and we are well advised not to leave our liberty in someone else's hands. Further, I would suggest that charity is a distinctly personal, not a collective, matter.

President Cleveland vetoed a $10,000 appropriation to purchase seed wheat for Texans who had suffered a drought. Included in his message was the point I wish to emphasize:

> Federal aid in such cases encourages the expectation of paternal care on the part of the Government and weakens the sturdiness of our national character, *while it prevents the indulgence among our people of that kindly sentiment and conduct which strengthens the bonds of a common brotherhood.*

Can any person relieve himself of charitable concerns without losing a priceless ingredient of individual emergence? Does not a growth of the spirit and soul of man require that a concern for others be retained for strictly personal attention? President Cleveland gave an affirmative answer to these questions, as do I.

There are, however, millions with "ability" who wish to make their own decisions as to how the fruits of their own labor should be expended. They have judgments concerning people in their own orbits, based on intimate experiences and relationships, a knowledge which no agency—governmental or private—can possibly possess. Are these persons to be deprived of their own funds and the practice of personal charity denied to them because some others wish the government to pre-empt the welfare activity?

You, for instance, wish to practice an act of charity. But this voluntary act—one of the highest expressions of a common brotherhood—is thwarted when your honestly acquired income is taken by government. What was yours has been arbitrarily declared not yours; a "social" claim on your labor has been decreed. Indeed, government now operates on the theory that it has a first lien on your income and capital; your freedom of choice is severely restricted. As a consequence, you are restrained from practicing your own religion should your religion call for a personal charity toward others. The state will practice charity for you. A common brotherhood, by some quirk of reasoning, is to become a collective act of compulsion!

Then again, you may want to save that part of your income over and above your requirements for current living. Perhaps you may wish to "stash it under the mattress"! Who has any moral right to forbid it? Do strangers who didn't earn it have any right, in logic and justice, to what you have earned?

When the responsibility for one's own welfare is surrendered to government, it follows that the authority to
conduct one's life goes where the responsibility is reposed.
This is a matter over which we have no choice; it is a law
of organization.

The idea set forth in the Declaration of Independence
that each person· has an inherent and inalienable right to
life becomes meaningless when a person loses the authority
for his own decisions and must act according to someone
else's dictates. Unless an individual is self-controlling, his
life is not truly his own. Before a life can be valued for its
own sake—not simply a means to someone else's goal—that
life must retain its own power to choose, along with its own
quality, its own dignity. Without self-power, there is no
basis for love, respect, and friendship, in short, a common
brotherhood; the powerless person becomes either a puppet
or an unwanted burden. Even a mother's love for an in-
valid child cannot exist unless it is voluntarily bestowed.
Aged persons and others who depend on the income of
others, confiscated by government, become mere numbers
in the confused statistics of political bureaus. Neither bureaus nor statistics have the capacity for charity or a common brotherhood.

Keeping in mind Emerson's accurate observation that the
end pre-exists in the means, it should be plain that the
evil means of confiscating income must lead to an evil end
to those who live on it.

Actually, we are dealing here with a problem arising
from a double standard of morality. Comparatively few
persons will take private property without the owner's con-

sent. We think of that as stealing and frown on the practice. Yet we will form a collective—politically group ourselves—and take billions in income without consent; we
thoughtlessly call it "doing good."

Doing politically what we reject doing individually in
no manner alters the immorality of the act; it merely legal-
izes the wrong and, thus, gains social absolution for the
criminal; giving it the political twist keeps one from being
tossed into jail! But to anyone who rejects the authoritarianism of a majority as much as that of a Stalin—to anyone who believes in the right to life and to one's honestly
acquired property—no moral absolution is gained by legislation.

Those who think only materialistically may argue that
the stealing of a loaf of bread is a loss to the person from
whom it is taken but a gain to the thief, if the thief "gets
away with it." This is an incorrect view. The person from
whom the loaf is taken loses only the loaf. But the one who
takes the loaf without the owner's consent loses not only the
respect of all who know him but loses also his integrity!
Man can never realize his creative potentialities without
integrity. This virtue lies at the root of emergence. To live
on loot appears to be no further removed from evil than
to take the loot.

Unless one believes in authoritarianism—that men
should lord it over men, that some fallible humans should
cast the rest of us in their little images—it is not possible
to see anything but harm done to the person in "need"
who is "aided" by taking the income of others without their
consent.

for the evidence is all about us and the reason plain to see.

Observe the profound change that comes over men when they are given power over others. When acting as responsible, self-controlled human beings—when attending to their own affairs—they were admirable both in their thinking and in their behavior. Now let power over others be vested in them. In due course—usually soon—they begin to think like authoritarians; they talk like authoritarians; they act like authoritarians; for, indeed, they are authoritarians. It is as if a chemical change had taken place in their persons.

Power or authority over the creative activities of others —that is, a responsibility for the creative behavior of others —is an assignment with an inevitably destructive consequence. Thus overburdened, a wielder of power eventually becomes intolerant, quick-tempered, irrational, disrespectful, and unrespected. How could he be expected to function as a strictly self-responsible individual under burdens which are not within his nature to shoulder?

Further, when in possession of political power over the creative actions of others, a fallible human being is almost certain to mistake this power for infallibility. The obeisance paid to a person in such authority, the drooling of the weak-willed who like to be led, the lies told by those who seek the favors he has the power to dispense—all these tend to aid and abet the process of his disintegration. It is not easy to reject flattery, regardless of its source. Indeed, the authoritarian loses his capacity to discriminate among sources. The mentality for directing others cannot simultaneously attend to the art of discrimination, the latter being a purely personal, introspective accomplishment of the intellect. This is why it is often said of authoritarians: "They surround themselves with 'yes men.'" They cannot abide dissenters; in running the lives of others, they must have helpers who agree. This process spells inferiority for the life that erroneously claims superiority.

Daily experience affords a clue as to what happens to the person who accepts dictatorship in any of its many forms. For example, observe two persons, with somewhat different views, rationally discussing some subject of common interest. Each offers the other his most intelligent ideas, thus encouraging friendship and mutual confidence. This setting, plus the privacy of the occasion, combine to elicit from each the best that he has to offer. The exchange of intellectual energies is mutually beneficial, and the awareness of this fact encourages thinking and understanding.

Now, place these same two individuals on a stage before a multitude, or place a microphone between them and announce that 50 million people are listening in. Instantly, their mental processes will change. Thoughtfulness and the desire to understand each other will all but cease. No longer will they function as receiving sets, drawing on the expansible capacities of their own and each other's intellects. They will become only sending stations; outgoing will take the place of intaking. And what they say will be influenced by how they think they sound to their audience and by their competition for applause. In short, they will become different persons because their psychological directives have changed. Those who forego self-improvement

CHAPTER 6

HOW SOCIALISM HARMS THE ECONOMY

OUR COUNTRY has stumbled into socialism during the past half century; by now—1964—we have adopted nearly all the things socialists have long urged upon us. A reading of the ten points in the *Communist Manifesto* confirms this. We who are aware of socialism's built-in destructiveness have watched this trend with apprehension. Foreseeing the end result, we are forever predicting, or warning against, the impending catastrophe which we think hangs over our economy.

Our dire predictions, however, fail to ring bells with many people. As a rule they are met by the rejoinder, "We never had it so good." And, so far as statistical measurements of material well-being are concerned, that claim appears to hold water. Prosperity, according to the National Bureau of Economic Research, is reported to have increased as follows:

> Today's national income of $2,300 per capita is double what it was (in constant dollars) forty years ago, and it is higher in the face of a 70 per cent increase in population and a 20 per cent reduction in the hours of paid work per capita.

Output per man hour has grown over the same period at the average annual rate of 2.6 per cent.

Today's higher income is more evenly distributed than the lower income of earlier years.

The economic difficulties of most everyone have been lessened through the establishment and broadening of various social welfare programs.

The four recessions we have encountered since World War II are among the milder in our history, which means an unusually long period free of serious depressions.[1]

Now, consider what has happened politically during this period. Statism, measured in terms of governmental expenditures per capita, has advanced from about $80 in the years just after World War I to more than $700 now.[2]

Small wonder, then, that most people, observing statism and prosperity advancing coincidentally over so long a period, conclude that the growth of statism is the cause of the increased prosperity! But if there is a positive correlation here, why not expand prosperity indefinitely by the mere expedient of increasing governmental expenditures? This absurdity needs no comment.

Nonetheless, it is true that the comeback, "We never had it so good," cannot easily be proved wrong statistically. A man leaping from an airplane at high altitude will, for a time in his fall, have the feeling of lying on a cloud. For a moment he would be warranted in exclaiming, "I've

---

[1] See *The Fortieth Annual Report* (1960), National Bureau of Economic Research, 261 Madison Avenue, New York, N. Y.

[2] How closely does this approach what we call the "authoritarian state"? One way to make an estimate is to measure governmental take of earned income. In 1917 it was less than 10 per cent. Today it is 36 per cent. We must keep in mind, however, that a state of dictatorship can exist prior to a 100 per cent take—perhaps at the halfway mark.

omy can long endure without a high degree of honesty. This is self-evident.

The degree of specialization in the U.S.A. today is without precedent in all history and, as a consequence, our dependence on each other is beyond the bounds of experience in this or any other country—ever! The question is, are we overly specialized and, thus, dangerously interdependent? I believe we are.

We are dangerously interdependent because so much of our specialization is unsound; it is not economic and natural but, instead, is governmentally forced and artificial. An economy founded on artificialities is in peril.

Economic specialization is the sturdy variety that blooms in the context of the peaceful, free, and unfettered market; it is the natural, technological outcropping of consumer requirements as reflected in voluntary, willing exchanges. Given these postulates, production, regardless of how specialized it is, generates its own purchasing power; balance is one of its built-in features.

Natural Specialization Welcomed

All advances in natural specialization improve the standard of living. It is true that interdependence increases with its growth, but without peril, for *economic interdependence is founded on consent*; the countless relationships are as firmly rooted in general harmony and acceptance as is the free exchange of 30 cents for a can of beans. In a free market transaction each party chalks up a gain, for each values what he receives more than what he gives; each party is in a thank-you mood. Check this assertion with your own shopping experiences.

Specialization of the free market variety develops an integrated interdependence because each person is his own man—the whole man; all the faculties are called upon in his interrelationships. The premium is on self-responsibility and honesty, these being the cohesive ingredients which make specialization and exchange a workable arrangement. To prove the validity of these affirmations, simply reflect on one's daily free market experiences with the purveyors of countless specializations: groceries by the hundreds, milk, school supplies, footwear, clothing, gas, electricity, on and on. The natural, peaceful, unfettered free market rewards—and gets—the honesty on which it relies.

Unnatural specialization, on the other hand, decreases rather than increases the standard of living. It does not have its origin in consent but in force. It is not the result of millions upon millions of judgments voluntarily rendered. It is, instead, founded on the whims, caprices—call these judgments, if you choose—of political persons and committees, the few who have gained power over the rest of us. When these political "ins" take over a sector of society, they remove it from the area where free choice may be exercised by the millions of "outs." Our faculties are less and less called upon; self-responsibility shifts to government or authoritarian responsibility—that of the political "ins." The premium on honesty disappears as prizes are given more and more for bending to expediency, trading influence and special privileges, log-rolling, and the like. From this turnabout, the individual tends to become

soldiers and policemen are possible, as history attests. Not every corner requires a stop light. It is easy to be talked into a battleship or a supersonic bomber binge. If the bureaucracy is not checked, it will tend to build, in the name of peace, a defense against every conceivable contingency—so much "security" that "the secured" are without resources—helpless and hopeless.

However, my aim in this chapter is not to discuss the merit of this or that type of forcible intervention; it is, rather, to suggest that there comes a point in unnatural specializations beyond which extension is impossible without the economy flying to pieces. Suppose that everyone were engaged in one of the nonexchangeable services such as designing and constructing devices to cushion the landing of TV sets on the moon!

Unmarketable Specialties

Regardless of the need some may see for government golf courses or price supports or compulsory education of children or federally financed hospitals or numberless other socializations, the fact is that tens of millions of American citizens in consequence are now engaged in and wholly dependent on *unmarketable* specializations—and the number grows apace. Increasingly, more and more millions are becoming dependent on such forced exchange of their unwanted specializations for those goods and services without which they cannot live. Even if the personal virtues of honesty and self-responsibility were at their highest state of development, instead of their present eroded state, such a system could not be made to work. Nothing but the total state—the police force in charge of everything—can cause us to exchange with each other goods and services none of us wants. And, the total state, as I have already tried to demonstrate, is noncreative. The possibility of a good economy disappears with the total state.

Bear in mind, when it comes to assessing prosperity and the state of the economy statistically, that dollars exchanged for unnatural specializations are counted as earned income precisely as if exchanged for natural specializations. This is a misleading fiction. For instance, there would be no decline in gross national product (GNP), as presently computed by government, if all of us indulged in unmarketable specializations provided, of course, that the state priced the specializations high enough and forced us to exchange them even while we are slowly starved!

Statistical measurements of economic well-being cannot gauge the honesty and self-responsibility of the citizens, nor can any statistics warn us when unnatural specializations are becoming top heavy; such is beyond the scope of statistical measurement.

If one wishes to know how socialism harms the economy, I suggest that much less attention be given to statistics than to the question: How much immoral action is being introduced into the economy? If socializing the means and the results of production is immoral, as I contend, then socialism harms the economy by introducing immorality into it. In short, watch moral trends, rather than numerical fictions, for danger signals.

what causes the expenses of government to be so high that they cannot be met by direct tax levies? At this level, the cause is more obscure. It is quite clear that expensive social-istic schemes do not have their origin in popular demand but, instead, are initiated by bureaucrats; imagined plights of minorities are dramatically portrayed and a demand for redress "whipped up."[1] But, more to our point, there are small yet powerful groupings of the electorate—pressure groups—who effectively petition government (1) to get them out of their own messes or (2) to obtain benefits at someone else's expense. At this depth there are causes ga-lore.

Pressure Tactics of Labor Unions

There are two reasons for considering labor unions as an example of the way pressure groups cause inflation and, thus, promote socialism (or, I might add, cause socialism and, thus, promote inflation!) First, by using the labor union example, we can demonstrate how businessmen, clergymen, and others bring on these twin destroyers.

Second, we can show that the "wage-spiral," coercively induced by unions, is not itself a cause of inflation. Un-derstanding how such accusations are incorrectly leveled at labor unions will afford a better look at the inflation-social-ism complex. Looking into labor union behavior is like looking into the mirror for millions of us. What we see is shocking!

---

[1] See "The Public Demands . . . ?" by Dr. Emerson P. Schmidt. *The Freeman*, August, 1964.

It can be truthfully said that *people* bring on both social-ism and inflation, but people do many other things besides. Thus, if we would stop inflation and thereby curb a major part of socialism, we should know which actions of people bring on inflation and which ones do not. In short, we need to know which one of the various labor union practices in-duces inflation. Otherwise, unions may be criticized on the wrong count while the critics innocently follow practices which bring on the very inflation they so stoutly deplore. We cannot hope to stop inflation until we gain some fa-miliarity with its causes—and the real cause will elude us as long as we chase fictitious ones.

The labor union critics who blame inflation on the in-cessant, persistent, coercive drives of labor unions for higher and higher wages are on the wrong track. Such coercion is not to be condoned, but it is not a cause of inflation. To explain: Suppose your gardener issues an ultimatum: either you pay him $100 a day from now on, or else he will quit—in which case he would use force if necessary to keep any other gardener from taking the job which he threatens to vacate (the labor union tactic, in principle). You are right if you condemn this action, but you are wrong if you call it a cause of inflation. Why? Because no dilution of the money supply (inflation) is induced by either your ac-ceptance or refusal of this demand. True, you may go broke if you accept, or he may become unemployed if you re-fuse, but that's all the economics there is to it—nothing happens to the money supply. Nor is the economics of it altered one whit if a labor union induces a million gar-deners to take similar action in unison. Inflation *is not* one

of the results. Such action as this merely creates an economic mess which the labor unions hasten to cover up.
They promote "full employment" programs (socialism)
which, to the casual observer, seem to absolve the unions
from having committed any uneconomic practices. *It is
these costly covering-up programs that bring on the inflation!*

Why Wages Rise

Like so many organizations, labor unions get blamed for
sins they never committed, receive absolution for follies of
their own making, have aims they cannot attain, and make
claims for deeds they never achieved. For example, unions
claim credit for raising wages. The truth is that unions
have had no more to do with the general level of wages
than with the level of the seven seas.[2] Admittedly, they
have succeeded in obtaining increases for some of their
members. And this has been not entirely at the expense
of nonmembers; their tactics have disemployed many of
their own members as well. In any event, their coercive
wage hikes have not caused inflation. It is the covering-up,
subsequent action that brings on inflation and makes the
growth of socialism a financial plausibility.

The actions of union members are based largely on the
thinking of their top officials. Much of their philosophy is
summarized in this sentence from an AFL-CIO pamphlet
(Publication No. 41) :

---

[2] For a confirmation of this fact see *Why Wages Rise* by F. A.
Harper (Irvington-on-Hudson, N. Y.: Foundation for Economic Education, Inc., 1957).

>Through their legislative activities, unions have continuously championed measures to improve governmental benefits for various groups of citizens, without regard to whether the beneficiaries are union members or not.

There may be less generosity in this doff of the hat to nonmembers than first meets the eye. One finds the unions, for instance, supporting more government aid to foreign countries, federal aid to education, more compulsory social security, government ownership of power and light facilities, federal aid to so-called distressed areas, and so on—all of these being part and parcel of government's guaranteed full employment program—the cover-up for uneconomic practices by labor unions.

Through Political Intervention

Labor unions are politically influential. In large measure, they obtain increased federal activity for projects they sponsor. Their coerced and uneconomic wage hikes cause unemployment; in short, their policies price workers out of the market. Then the unions throw their enormous political influence behind federal urban renewal and other "full employment" projects which, in turn, cost billions of dollars, making for governmental costs that cannot possibly be financed by direct tax levies. *And this is how labor unions cause inflation and socialism!*

In principle, if not in degree, the social action program of the National Council of Churches resembles the labor unions' program—the assumption by government of more and more responsibility for the welfare of the people. The

National Council of Churches is influential. The government activities it sponsors carry enormous costs. *This is how the N.C.C. causes inflation and socialism!*

And, chambers of commerce? Only a few in the whole nation have refrained from seeking federal aid for local roads, hospitals, airports, and so forth. Chambers of commerce have political influence. The "benefits" they advocate and achieve cost money. *This is how chambers of commerce cause inflation and socialism!*

Millions of citizens from all walks of life cause inflation in the very same manner. And all of them, along with labor unions, the N.C.C., chambers of commerce, and thousands of other organizations loudly decry inflation and demand that the fire be put out as they more or less innocently add fuel to it!

Were we to explore any deeper, we should have to inquire into the cause of the lax dispersal of the unlimited billions of dollars that government so easily grants to any and all pressure-group beggars. Why this Aladdin's Lamp, the slightest rubbing of which yields handouts without limit? Why, in Congress, is the question seldom asked any more, "Where's the money coming from?" The cause of this fiscal irresponsibility is complex indeed, but it has to do with that dearth of economic understanding which allows people to believe they can pay bills by "watering" the medium of exchange, with a crack-up in our educational system, an inability to see and think long-range, a breakdown in integrity, and a striking perversion of the ideal of statesmanship.

CHAPTER 8

APPOINT A COMMITTEE!

THE PRACTICE of committees, boards, or councils presuming to represent the views of vast constituencies occurs in educational and religious associations, in trade and commercial organizations, indeed in any segment of society where there is the propensity to organize.

While there are daily examples by the thousands of this "thinking by proxy," one that stood out, and about which many are aware, had to do with a debate between the National Council of Churches and its erstwhile National Lay Committee. Their debate brought into focus a fault that may well lie at the root of unpeaceful socialism. It had to do with the propriety of the N.C.C.'s seeming to speak for 35,800,000 Protestants on social, political, and economic questions. The N.C.C. argued affirmatively, the Lay Committee negatively.[1]

Leo Tolstoy made the point I wish to examine:

From the day when the first members of councils placed exterior authority higher than interior, that is to say, recognized the decisions of men united in councils as more important and more sacred than reason and conscience; *on that day began*

---

[1] *U.S. News and World Report,* February 3, 1956, pp. 43-46.

lies that caused the loss of millions of human beings and which continue their unhappy work to the present day.[2]

Tolstoy's is a striking statement. Is it possible that there is something of a wholly destructive nature which has its source in council, or in group, or in committee-type action? Can this sort of thing generate lies that actually cause the loss of "millions of human beings"? And, as I believe, aid and abet socialism in this bad bargain?

Any reasonable clue to the unhappy state of our affairs merits investigation. Two world wars that settled nothing, but added to the difficulties of avoiding even worse ones; men of doubtful character rising to positions of power over millions of other men; freedom to produce, to trade, to travel disappearing from the earth; everywhere the fretful talk of security as insecurity daily becomes more evident; suggested solutions to problems made of the stuff that gave rise to the problems in the first place; the tragic spectacle, even here in America, of any one of many union labor leaders being able, at will, to control a strategic part of the complex exchange machinery on which the livelihood of all depends; these and other perplexities of import combine to raise a tumultuous "why," and to hasten the search for answers.

Strange how wide and varied the search, as though we intuitively knew the cause to lie in some elusive, hidden, unnoticed error; thousands of not too well tutored folks trying to find light in difficult and erudite tomes, other thousands groping in quiet reflection for answers.

---

[2] Leo Tolstoy, *The Law of Love and the Law of Violence* (New York: Rudolph Field, 1948), p. 26.

Yes, the search is on for the errors and their answers—for the affair is serious; the stake is life itself. And the error or errors, it is agreed at least among the serious-minded, may well be found deep in the thoughts and behaviors of men, even of well-intentioned men. Anyway, everything and everyone is suspect. And, why not? When there is known to be a culprit and the culprit is not identified, what other scientifically sound procedure is there?

". . . on that day began lies . . . " That is a thought which deserves reflection. Obviously, if everything said or written were lies, then truth or right principles would be unknown. Subtract all knowledge of right principles, and there would not be chaos among men; there would be no men at all.

If half of everything said or written were lies . . . ? What then?

Principled Behavior

Human life is dependent not only on the knowledge of right principles but relies, also, on actions in accord with right principles. However, the nearest that any person can get to right principles—truth—is that which his highest personal judgment dictates as right. Beyond that, one cannot go or achieve. *Truth, then, as nearly as any individual can express it, is in strict conformity with this inner, personal dictate of rightness.*

The accurate representation of this inner, personal dictate is intellectual integrity. It is the expressing, living, acting of such truth as any given person possesses. Inaccurate representation of what one believes to be right is

untruth. It is a lie in the high level sense of the word, the
type of lie Tolstoy vetoed and deplored.

Attaining knowledge of right principles is an infinite
process. It is a never-ending performance, a perpetual hatching, a goal to be pursued but never attained. Intellectual
integrity—the accurate reflection of highest personal judgment—on the other hand, is undeniably within the reach
of all. Thus, the very best we can ever hope to do with
ourselves is to project ourselves at our best. To do otherwise is to tell a lie. To tell lies is to deny such truth as
is known, and to deny truth is to destroy ourselves and
others.

It would seem to follow, then, that if we would find the
origin of lies, we might put the spotlight on the genesis of
our troublous times. This is why it seems appropriate to
accept Tolstoy's statement as a working hypothesis and to
examine the idea that lies begin when men accept "decisions
of men united in councils as more important and more
sacred than reason and conscience." For, certainly, today,
many of the decisions which guide national and world
policy spring from "men united in councils."

In what manner, then, do the "decisions of men united
in councils" tend to initiate lies? A long experience with
these arrangements suggests to me that there are several
ways.

Mob Action Analyzed

The first way has to do with a strange and what must be
an unconscious behavior of men in association. Consider
the lowest form of association, the mob. It is a loose and

wholly emotional type of gathering. The mob will tar and feather, burn at the stake, string up by the neck; in short, murder! But dissect this association, pull it apart for a careful view, investigate its members. Each person, very often, is a God-fearing, home-loving, wouldn't-kill-a-fly type of individual.

What happens then? What causes persons in a mob to behave as they do? What accounts for the distinction between these persons acting as self-responsible individuals and these very same persons acting in mob-type committee?

Perhaps it is this: These persons, when in mob association, and perhaps at the instigation of a demented leader, lose the self-disciplines which guide them in individual or self-controlled action; thus, the evil which is in each person is released, for there is some evil in each of us. In this situation, no one of the mobsters consciously assumes the *personal* guilt for what is thought to be a collective act but, instead, puts the onus of it on an irresponsible abstraction—the mob.

I may appear to be unfair in relating mob association to association in general. In all but one respect, yes. But in this single exception there is a striking similarity.

Individuals support proposals in association that they would never propose on their own responsibility. Persons of normal veracity, by any of the common standards of honesty, will join as a board or a committee to sponsor legal thievery, for instance—they will urge the use of the political means to exact the fruits of the labor of others to benefit themselves, their groups, their community or, to put it bluntly, their mob.

Joe Doakes Seeks Entry

Imagine this: Joe Doakes passed away, his spirit floating to the Pearly Gates. In response to a knock, Saint Peter appeared and inquired:

"Who are you, may I ask?"

"My name is Joe Doakes, sir."

"Where are you from?"

"I am from Robinhoodsville, U.S.A."

"Why are you here?"

"I plead admittance."

Saint Peter scanned his scroll and said:

"Yes, Joe, your name appears on my list but I cannot admit you."

"Why not, pray tell?"

"You stole money from millions of others, including widows and orphans."

"You must have me confused with someone else; I had the reputation of being the most honest man in my community."

"You may have had that reputation among men, but they did not see through the nature of your actions. You see, Joe, you were a member, a financial supporter, and once on the Board of Directors of the Robinhoodsville Chamber of Commerce, the most influential committee in your town. You folks, gathered in council, advocated and obtained a municipal golf course. That project took from the livelihood of others, including widows and orphans, in order that a hundred or so golfers might enjoy the sport with little cost to themselves."

"But Saint Peter, the Robinhoodsville Chamber of Commerce took that action, not your humble applicant, Joe Doakes."

Saint Peter scanned his scroll again, slowly raised his head and said somewhat sadly:

"Joe, the Robinhoodsville Chamber of Commerce is not on my list, nor any foundation, nor any church, nor any trade association, nor any labor union, nor any P.T.A., nor any committee. All I have on my scroll are individuals, *just individuals*."

It ought to be obvious that we as individuals do stand responsible for our actions regardless of any wishes to the contrary and irrespective of the devices we try to arrange to avoid personal responsibility. Actions of the group—council or committee—insofar as they are not accurate reflections of the participating individuals, must be classified as lies.

The Art of Compromise

Another way that lies are initiated by the "decisions of men united in councils" inheres in commonly accepted committee practices. Here is a committee which has been assigned the task of preparing a report on what should be done about rent control. The first member is devoted to the welfare-state idea and believes that rents should forever be controlled by governmental fiat. The second member is a devotee of the voluntary society with its free market economy, and a government of strictly limited powers. He, therefore, believes all remaining rent control should be abolished immediately. The third member believes that rent control is wrong but that decontrol should be effected gradually, over a period of years.

This not uncommon situation is composed of men honestly holding three different and irreconcilable beliefs. Yet, a report is expected and, under the customary committee theory and practice, is usually forthcoming. What shall they do? Is there some compromise not too disagreeable to any one of the three committeemen? For instance, why not recommend that landlords be permitted by government to increase rents by no more than 15 per cent? Agreed!

In this hypothetical case—in no way at odds with common practice—the recommendation is a fabrication. Truth, as understood by any one of the three, has no spokesman; it has been miserably distorted. By any reasonable definition, a lie has been told.

This example (numberless variations could be cited) suggests only the nature of the lie in embryo. It is interesting to see what becomes of it.

Behind the Committee

Not all bodies called committees are true committees, a phase of the discussion that will be dealt with later. However, the true committee—an arrangement which calls for resolutions in accord with what a majority of the members are willing to say in concert—is but the instigator of fabrications yet more pronounced. The committee, for the most part, presupposes another larger body to which its recommendations are made.

These larger bodies have a vast, a very nearly all-inclusive, range in present-day American life: the neighborhood development associations; the small town and big city chambers of commerce; the regional and national trade associations; the P.T.A.'s; labor unions organized vertically to encompass crafts and horizontally to embrace industries; farmers' granges and co-ops; medical and other professional societies; ward, precinct, county, state, and national organizations of political parties; government councils, from the local police department to the Congress of the United States; the United Nations; thousands and tens of thousands of them, every citizen embraced by several of them and millions of citizens embraced by scores of them; most of them resolving to act as groups, as "men united in councils."

These associational arrangements divide quite naturally into two broad classes: (1) those that are of the voluntary type, the kind to which we pay dues if we want to, and (2) those that are a part of government, the kind to which we pay taxes whether we want to or not. For the purpose of this critique, emphasis will be placed on the voluntary type.

Now, it is not true, nor is it here pretended, that every associational resolution originates in distortions of personal conceptions of what is right. But any one of the millions of citizens who participate in these associations has, by experience, learned how extensive these fabrications are. As a matter of fact, there has developed a rather large acceptance of the notion that wisdom can be derived from the averaging of opinions, provided there are enough of them. The quantitative theory of wisdom, so to speak!

The Deception Extended

If one will concede that the aforementioned committee characteristics and council behaviors are perversions of truth, it becomes interesting to observe the manner of their extension—to observe how the lie is compounded.

Analyzed, it runs something like this: An association takes a position on some issue and claims or implies that it speaks for its 1,000,000 members. It is possible, of course, that each of the million members agrees with the stand taken by the association. But in all probability, this is an untruthful claim for the following reasons:

1. If every member were actually polled on the issue, and the majority vote were accepted as the association's position, there is no certainty that more than 500,001 persons agreed with the position claimed to be that of the 1,000,000.

2. If not all members were polled, or not all were at the meeting where the voting took place, there is only the certainty that a majority of those voting favored the position of the association—still claimed to be the position of 1,000,-000 members. If a quorum should be 100, there is no certainty that more than 51 persons agreed with the position.

3. It is still more likely that the opinion of the members was not tested at all. The officers, or some committee, or some one person may have determined the stand of the association. Then there is no certainty that more than one person (or a majority of the committee) favored the association's position.

4. And, finally, if that person should be dishonest—that is, untrue to that which he personally believes to be right, either by reason of ulterior motives, or by reason of anticipating what the others might approve—then, it is pretty certain that the resolution did not even originate in a single honest opinion.

A personal experience will highlight the point I am trying to make. The economist of a national association and I were breakfasting, just after V-J Day. Wage and price controls were still in effect. The economist opened our dialogue:

> "I have just written a report on wage and price controls which I think you will like."
>
> "Why do you say you *think* I will like it? Why don't you say you *know* I will like it?"
>
> "Well, I—er—hedged a little on rent controls."
>
> "You don't believe in rent controls. Why did you hedge?"
>
> "Because the report is as strong as I think our Board of Directors will adopt."
>
> "As the economist, isn't it your duty and responsibility to state that which you believe to be right? If the Board Members want to take a wrong action, let them do so and bear the responsibility for it."

Actually, what did happen? The Board adopted that report as written by the economist. It was represented to a committee of the Congress as the considered opinion of the constituency of that association. Many of the members believed in the immediate abolishment of rent control. Yet, they were reported as believing otherwise—and paying dues to be thus represented. By supporting this procedure with their membership and their money, they were as responsible as though they had gone before the Congress and told the lie themselves.

In order to avoid the twofold dishonesty in this situation, the spokesman of that association would have had to tell the whole truth to the congressional committee. It would have been like this:

> "This report was adopted by our Board of Directors, 35 of the 100 being present. The vote was 18 in favor, 12 against; 5 did not vote. The report itself was written by the association's economist, *but he does not believe it is right.*"

Such honesty or exactness is more the exception than the rule, as everyone who has had experience in associational work can attest. What really happens is a misrepresentation of concurrence, a misorganized way of lying about how many of any group stand for what. Truth, such as is known, is seldom spoken. It is warped into a misleading distortion. It is obliterated by this process of the majority speaking for the minority, more often by the minority speaking for the majority, sometimes by one dishonest opportunist speaking for thousands. Truth, such as is known —the best judgments of individuals—for the most part, goes unrepresented, unspoken.

This, then, is the thread out of which much of local, national, and world policy is being woven. Is it any wonder that many citizens are confused?

Three questions are in order:

(1) What is the reason for all these troubles with truth?

(2) What should we do about these associational difficulties?

(3) Is there a proper place for associational activity as relating to important issues?

The Reasons Examined

As emphasized in the previous chapter, pointing out causes is a hazardous venture; as one ancient sage put it, "Even from the beginnings of the world descends a chain of causes." Thus, for the purpose of this critique, it would be folly to attempt more than casual reference to some of our own recent experiences.

First, there appears to be no widespread, lively recognition of the fact that conscience, reason, knowledge, integrity, fidelity, and other virtues are the distinctive and exclusive properties of individual persons.

Somehow, there follows from this lack of recognition the mischievous notion that wisdom can be derived by pooling the conclusions of a sufficient number of persons, even though no one of them has applied his faculties to the problem in question. From this premise, the imagination begins to ascribe personal characteristics to a collective—the committee, council, association—as though the collective could think, judge, know, or assume responsibility. With this as a notion, there is the inclination to substitute the "decisions of men united in councils" for the reason and conscience of persons. The individual feels relieved of personal responsibility and thus gives no real thought to the matter in question.

Second, there is an almost blind faith in the efficacy and rightness of majority decision, as though the mere preponderance of opinion were the device for determining what is right. This thinking is consistent with and a part of the "might makes right" doctrine.

Third, we have carried the division-of-labor practice to such a high point in this country, and with such good effect in standard-of-living benefits, that we seem to have forgotten that the practice has any limitations. Many of us, in our voluntary associational activities, have tried to delegate moral and personal responsibilities to these associational abstractions.

As a consequence, our policies and public positions are

void of reason and conscience. These massive quantities of unreasoned collective declarations and resolutions have the power to inflict damage but are generally useless in conferring understanding. So much for causes.

Do Not Participate!

Next, what can be done about these associational difficulties? I can give only my own answer. I do not know what *our* attitude should be, but only what *mine* is! *It is to have no part in any association whatsoever which takes actions implicating me, for which I am not ready and willing to accept personal responsibility.*[3]

Put it this way: If I am opposed, for instance, to spoliation—legal plunder—I am not going to risk being reported in its favor. This is a matter having to do with morals, and moral responsibility is strictly a personal affair. In this and like areas, I prefer to speak for myself. I do not wish to carry the division-of-labor idea, the delegation of authority, to this untenable extreme.

One friend who shares these general criticisms objects to the course I have taken. He argues that he must remain in associations which persist in misrepresenting him in order to influence them for the better. If one accepts this view, how can he avoid "holing up" with every evil to be found, anywhere? How can one lend support to an agency which lies about his convictions and avoid living a lie in

---

[3] This determination of mine does not refer to membership in or support of either of the two major political parties. What I consider to be an appropriate role concerning partisan politics is reserved for the next chapter.

the process? If to stop such evil in others one has to indulge in evil, it seems evident that evil will soon become
universal. The alternative? Stop lending a hand to the
doing of evil! This at least has the virtue of lessening the
evildoers by one. Furthermore, were there a record of the
men who have wrought the greatest changes for good in
the world, I am certain that the ones who acted on their
own responsibility would top the ones who acted in committees.

How Associations May Help

Now the third question, "Is there a proper place for
associational activity as relating to important public issues?" There is.

The bulk of activities conducted by many associations
is as businesslike, as economical, as appropriate to the division-of-labor process, as is the organization of specialists to
bake bread or to make automobiles. It is not this vast number of useful service activities that is in question.

The phase of committee activities which I see as the
cause of so much mischief has to do with a technique, a
plausible but insidious method by which reason and conscience—the repositories of such truths as we possess—
are not only robbed of incentive for improvement but are
actually used for fabrications, which are then represented
as the convictions of persons who hold no such convictions.
No better device for the promotion of socialism was ever
invented!

It was noted above that not all bodies called committees
are true committees, a true committee being an arrange-

ment by which a number of persons bring forth a report consistent with what the majority is willing to state in concert. The true committee is part and parcel of the "majority is right" line of thought—or lack of thought.

The alternative arrangement, on occasion referred to as a committee, may include the same set of men. The distinction is that the responsibility and the authority for a study is vested not in the collective, the set of men, but in one person, preferably the one most skilled in the subject at issue. The others serve not as decision makers but as consultants. The one person exercises his own judgment as to the suggestions to be incorporated or omitted. The report is his and is presented as his, with such acknowledgments of assistance and concurrence as the facts warrant. In short, the responsibility for the study and the authority to conduct it are reposed where responsibility and authority are capable of being exercised—in an individual. This arrangement takes full advantage of the skills and specialties of all parties concerned. The tendency here is toward an intellectual leveling-up, whereas with the true committee the tendency is toward irresponsibility. The first principle of any successful organizational arrangement is: always keep responsibility and authority commensurate and in balance.

On occasion, associations are formed for a particular purpose and supported by those who are like-minded as to that purpose. As long as the associational activities are limited to the stated purpose and as long as the members remain like-minded, the danger of misrepresentation is removed.

It is the multipurposed association, the one that potentially may take a "position" on a variety of subjects, particularly subjects relating to the rights or the property of others—moral questions—where misrepresentation is not only possible but almost certain. Merely keep in mind the nature of a committee.

The remedy here, if a remedy can be put into effect, is for the association to quit taking "positions" except on such rare occasions as unanimous concurrence is manifest, or *except as the exact and precise degree and extent of concurrence is represented.* Were the whole truth told about the genesis of and the concurrence in most committee reports, their destiny would be the wastebasket.

The Strength of the Individual

The alternative to associational "positions" is individual membership positions, that is, using the associational facilities to service the members: provide headquarters and meeting rooms where members may assemble in free association, exchange ideas, take advantage of the knowledge of others, learn of each other's experiences and thoughts. In addition, let the association be staffed with research experts and a competent secretariat, having on hand a working library and other aids to learning. Then, let the members speak or write or act as individual persons! Indeed, this is the real, high purpose of voluntary associations.

The practical as well as the ethical advantages of this suggested procedure may not at first be apparent. Imagine Patrick Henry having said:

"I move that this convention go on record as insisting that we prefer death to slavery." ‗‗

Now, suppose that the convention had adopted that motion. What would have been its force? Certainly almost nothing as compared to Patrick Henry's ringing words:

"*I* know not what course *others* may take; but as for *me,* give *me* liberty or give *me* death!" (Italics mine)

This was not a case of Patrick Henry's trying to decide for anyone else. His listeners were invited to consider only what he had decided for himself, and thus could weigh, more favorably, the merits of emulation. No convention, no association, no "decisions of men united in councils" could have said such a thing in the first place; and second, anything the members might have said in concert could not have matched the force of this personal declaration. Third, had the convention been represented in any such sentiments, it is likely that misrepresentations would have been involved.

A moment's reflection on the words of wisdom that have come down to us throughout all history, the words and works that have had the power to live, the words and works around which we have molded much of our lives, must reveal that they are the words and works of persons— not of collectives or sets of men, not what men have uttered in concert, not the "decisions of men united in councils."

In short, if advancement of what's right is the objective, then the decision-of-men-united-in-council practice could well be abandoned on the basis of its impracticality—if for no higher reason. Conceded, it can do mischief; it is also an utter waste of time in the creative areas, that is, for the advancement of truth.

The reasons for the impracticality of this device in the creative areas seem clear. Each of us when seeking perfection, whether of the spirit, of the intellect, or of the body, looks not to his inferiors but to his betters, not to those who self-appoint themselves as his betters, but to those who, in his own humble judgment, are his betters. Experience has shown that such perfection as there is exists in individuals, not in the lowest common-denominator expressions of a collection of individuals. Perfection emerges with the clear expression of personal faiths—the truth as it is known, not with the confusing announcement of verbal amalgams—lies.

". . . on that day began lies that caused the loss of millions of human beings and which continue their unhappy work to the present day." The evidence, if fully assembled and correctly presented, would, no doubt, convincingly affirm Tolstoy's observation. We have, in this process, the promoter of socialism and the enemy of peace.

How to stop this type of lie? It is simply a matter of personal determination and a resolve to act and speak in strict accord with one's own inner, personal dictate of what is right—and for each of us to see to it that no other man or set of men is given our permission to represent us otherwise.

CHAPTER 9

REGARDLESS OF CHOICE, VOTE!

IN THE PREVIOUS CHAPTER I vowed never to support any organization which would take positions representing me, which positions I would not willingly (peacefully) stand personally responsible for. In short, I object to organizations that claim a consensus that does not exist—a false reporting of agreement growing out of committee action.

It is logical for anyone to inquire, "Well, what about support of and membership in one of the two major political parties? Would you go so far as to take part in neither of these? You would vote for the candidate of one or the other party, regardless of positions, wouldn't you?" These are good questions and deserve a careful answer, though I am not suggesting that anyone else adopt my view.

According to *The Columbia Encyclopedia,* "the existence of only two major parties, as in most English-speaking countries, presupposes general public agreement on constitutional questions and on the aims of government." This idea is fundamental to my thesis. Under such agreeable circumstances, each party keeps a check on the other, thus giving assurance that neither party will step out of the bounds that have been agreed upon.

Let it be re-emphasized that the two-party system (1)

presupposes a general agreement on constitutional questions and the aims of government and (2) aims at, if it does not presuppose, honest candidates contending for office *within the framework of that constitution.* In this kind of political order, each office seeker is supposed to present fairly his own capabilities as related to the agreed-upon framework, voting being for the purpose of deciding which candidate is more competent for that limited role.

Clearly, the theory as originally conceived did not intend that the positions of candidates should be a response to voter opinion polls concerning the content or meaning of the constitution and the aims of government. If voters could thus reshape or reform the boundaries of government at will, there would be no need of candidates. Far less costly and more efficient would be the purchase of an electronic computer into which voter opinions and caprices would be continually fed; it could spew out altered constitutions and governmental purposes every second!

If there were "a general public agreement on constitutional questions and on the aims of government," and if candidates were vying with each other for office solely on their competency to perform within this framework, I would have no comment. But there is little contemporary agreement as to constitutional questions and the aims of government! Name a point that can now be presupposed. Both the questions and the aims are at sixes and sevens.

And as to candidates—with a few notable exceptions—they no longer contend with each other as to their competence to serve within a generally accepted framework but, instead:

(1) they compete to see which one can come up with the most popular alteration of the framework, and

(2) they compete to see which one can get himself in front of the most popular voter grab bag in order to stand four-square for some people's supposed right to other people's income.

The upshot of this political chaos is that voters are seldom given the chance to decide on the basis of competency but have only the choice of deciding between opportunists or, a better term, *trimmers*. This changed situation does, indeed, call for comments about political party membership and voting.

Despite the respectability of the two-party theory, its practice has "come a cropper." Today, trimming is so much in vogue that often a voter cannot cast a ballot except for one of two trimmers. Heard over and over again is the apology, "Well, the only choice I had was to vote for the lesser of two evils. I had to vote for one of them, didn't I?" A moral tragedy is implicit in this confession, as well as a political fallacy; in combination they must eventually lead to economic disaster.

I. THE MORAL TRAGEDY

It is morally tragic whenever a citizen's only choice is between two wrongdoers—that is, between two trimmers.

A trimmer, according to the dictionary, is one who changes his opinions and policies to suit the occasion. In contemporary political life, he is any candidate whose position on issues depends solely on what he thinks will have most voter appeal. He ignores the dictates of his higher conscience, trims his personal idea of what is morally right, tailors his stand to the popular fancy. Integrity, the accurate reflection in word and deed of that which is thought to be morally right, is sacrificed to expediency.

These are severe charges, and I do not wish to be misunderstood. One of countless personal experiences will help clarify what is meant: A candidate for Congress sat across the desk listening to my views about limited government. At the conclusion of an hour's discussion he remarked, "I am in thorough accord with your views; you are absolutely right. But I couldn't get elected on any such platform, so I shall represent myself as holding views other than these." He might as well have added, "I propose to bear false witness."

No doubt the candidate thought, on balance, that he was justified, that The Larger Good would be better served were he elected—regardless of how untruthfully he represented his position—than were he to stand for his version of the truth and go down to defeat.

This candidate is "a mixed-up kid." His values are topsy-turvy, as the saying goes. In an egotism that has no parallel, he puts his election to office above honesty. Why, asks the responsible voter, should I endorse dishonesty by voting for such a candidate? He has, on his own say-so, forsworn virtue by insisting on bearing false witness. Does he think his ambition for office is right because he needs a job? Then let him seek employment where want of principle is less harmful to others. Or, is his notion of rightness based on how much the rest of us would benefit by having him as our representative? What? A person with-

out moral scruple representing us in Congress! The role
of the legislator is to secure our rights to life, liberty,
and property—that is, to protect us against fraud, violence, predation, and misrepresentation (false witness).
Would our candidate have us believe that "it takes a crook
to catch a crook"?

Such righteousness or virtue as exists in the mind of
man does not and cannot manifest itself in the absence of
integrity—the honest, accurate reflection in deeds of one's
beliefs. Without this virtue the other virtues must lie dor-
mant and unused. What else remains? It is doubtful if
anything contributes more to the diseased condition of
society than the diminishing practice of integrity.

Those of us who attach this much importance to integrity must perforce construe trimming as evil. Therefore,
when both candidates for public office are judged to be
trimmers, the one who trims less than the other is often
regarded as "the lesser of two evils." But, is he really? It
must be conceded that there are gradations of wrongdoing: killing is worse than stealing, and perhaps stealing
is worse than covetousness. At any rate, if wrongdoing is
not comparative, then it is self-evident that the best of
us are just as evil as the worst of us; for man is fallible,
all men!

Degrees of Evil

While categories of wrongdoing are comparative, it does
not follow that wrong deeds within any given category of
evil are comparative. For instance, it is murder whether

one man is slain, or two. It is stealing whether the amount is ten cents or a thousand dollars. And, a lie is a lie whether told to one person or to a million. "Thou shalt not kill"; "Thou shalt not steal"; "Thou shalt not bear false witness" are derived from principles. Principles do not permit of compromise; they are either adhered to or surrendered.

Is trimming comparative? Can one trimmer be less at fault than another trimmer? Does the *quantity* of trimming have anything whatsoever to do with the matter? Or, rather, is this not a question of *quality* or character? To trim is to ignore the dictates of higher conscience; it is to take flight from integrity. Is not the candidate who will trim once for one vote likely to trim twice for more votes? Does he not demonstrate by any single act of trimming, regardless of how minor, that he stands ready to abandon the dictates of conscience for the place he seeks in the political sun? Does not the extent or quantity of trimming merely reflect a judgment as to how much trimming is expedient?

If the only question at issue is whether a candidate will trim at all, then trimming is not comparative; thus, it would be incorrect to report, "I cast my ballot for the lesser of two evils." Accuracy would require, "I felt there was no choice except to cast a ballot for one of two men, both of whom have sacrificed integrity for the hope of votes."

We must not, however, heap all our condemnation on candidates who trim. There would be no such candidates were it not for voters who trim. Actually, when we find only trimmers to vote for, most of us are getting what we deserve. The trimmers who succeed in offering themselves as candidates are, by and large, mere reflections of irresponsible citizenship—that is, of neglected thinking, study, education, vigilance. Candidates who trim and voters who trim are each cause and each effect; they feed on each other. *When the worst get on top it is because there are enough of the worst among us to put them there.*

To repeat, when one must choose between men who forsake integrity, the situation is tragic, and there is little relief at the polling level except as candidates of integrity may be encouraged by voters of integrity. Impractical idealism? Of course not! Read Edmund Burke, one of the great statesmen of all time, addressing his constituency:

> But his [the candidate's] unbiased opinion, his mature judgment, his enlightened conscience, he ought not to sacrifice to you, to any man, or to any set of men living. These he does not derive from your pleasure—no, nor from the law and the Constitution. They are a trust from Providence, for the abuse of which he is deeply answerable. Your representative owes you, not his industry only, but his judgment; and he betrays instead of serving you, if he sacrifices it to your opinion.

II. THE POLITICAL FALLACY

Is it fallacious to believe that responsible citizenship requires casting a ballot for one or the other of two candidates, *regardless of how far the candidates have departed from moral rectitude?*

Before trying to arrive at an answer, let us reflect on the reason why the so-called duty of casting a ballot, regardless of circumstance, is so rarely questioned. Quite obviously, the duty to vote is one of those sanctified institutions, such as motherhood, which is beyond criticism. The obligation to vote at any and all elections, whatever the issues or personalities, is equated with responsible citizenship. Voting is deeply embedded in the democratic mores as a duty, and one does not affront the mores without the risk of scorn. To do so is to "raise the dead": it is to resurrect questions that have been settled once and for all; it is to throw doubt on custom, tradition, orthodoxy, the folkways!

Yet any person who is conscious of our rapid drift toward the omnipotent state can hardly escape the suspicion that there may be a fault in our habitual way of looking at things. If the suspicion be correct, then it would be fatal never to examine custom. So, let us bring the sanctity of voting into the open and take a hard look at it, in a spirit of inquiry rather than advocacy.

Now for the hard look: Where is the American who will argue that responsible citizenship would require casting a ballot if a Hitler and a Stalin were the opposing candidates? "Ah," some will complain, "you carry the example to an absurdity." Very well, let us move closer to home and our own experience.

Government in the U.S.A. has been pushed far beyond its proper sphere. The Marxian tenet, "from each according to ability, to each according to need," backed by the armed force of the state, has become established policy. This is partly rationalized by something called "the new economics." Within this kind of political framework, it

is to be expected that one candidate will stand for the coercive expropriation of the earned income of all citizens,
giving the funds thus gathered to those in groups A, B,
and C. Nor need we be surprised that his opponent differs
from him only in advocating that the loot be given to
those in groups X, Y, and Z. Does responsible citizenship
require casting a ballot for either of these political plunderers? The citizen has no significant moral choice but only
an immoral choice in the event he has joined the unholy
alliance himself and thinks that one of the candidates will
deliver some of the largess to him or to a group he favors.
In the latter case, the problem is not one of responsible
citizenship but of irresponsible looting.

The Duty to Vote

Does responsible citizenship require voting for irresponsible candidates? To ballot in favor of irresponsible
candidates as though it were one's duty is to misconstrue
the meaning of duty. To cast a ballot for a trimmer, because no man of integrity is offering himself, does as
much as one can with a ballot to encourage other trimmers to run for office. Can anyone conceive of any element
of protest in such balloting? To vote for a trimmer goes
further: it would seem to urge, as strongly as one can at
the polls, that men of integrity not offer themselves as candidates.

What would happen if we adopted as a criterion: *Never
vote for a trimmer!* Conceding a generous liberality in defining trimmers, millions of us would not cast ballots.

Would the end result of this substantial, nonviolent protest, this large-scale demonstration of "voting by turning our backs," compound our problem? It is difficult to imagine how it could. For a while we would continue to get what we now have: a high percentage of trimmers and plunderers in public office, men who promise privileges in exchange for ballots—and freedom. In time, however, this silent but eloquent refusal to participate might conceivably improve the situation. Men of integrity and high moral quality—statesmen—might show forth and, if so, we could add their numbers to the few now in evidence.

Would a return to integrity by itself solve our problem? No, for many men of integrity do not understand freedom; or, if they do, are not devoted to it. But it is only among men of integrity that any solution can *begin* to take shape. Such men, at least, will do the right as they see the right; they tend to be teachable. Trimmers and plunderers, on the other hand, are the enemies of morality and freedom by definition; their motivations are below the level of principles; they cannot see beyond the emoluments of office.[1]

Here is a thought to weigh: If respect for a candidate's integrity were widely adopted as a criterion for casting a ballot, millions of us, as matters now stand, would not cast ballots. Yet, in a very practical sense, would not those of us who protest in this manner be voting? Certainly, we would be counted among that growing number who, by

---

[1] If it be conceded that the role of government is to secure "certain unalienable rights, that among them are the right to life, liberty, and the pursuit of happiness," by what stretch of the imagination can this be achieved when we vote for those who are openly committed to *unsecuring* these rights?

our conscious and deliberate inaction, proclaim that we have no party. What other choice have we at the polling level? Would not this encourage men of statesmanlike qualities to offer themselves in candidacy?

The Sanctity of the Ballot

Why is so much emphasis placed upon voting as a responsibility of citizenship?[2] Why the sanctity attached to voting? Foremost, no doubt, is a carry-over from an all-but-lost ideal in which voting is associated with making choices between honest beliefs, between candidates of integrity. We tend to stick with the form regardless of what has happened to the substance. Further, this attitude toward voting may derive in part from the general tendency to play the role of Robin Hood, coupled with a reluctance to acknowledge this practice for what it is. Americans, at least, have some abhorrence of forcibly taking from the few and giving to the many without any sanction whatsoever. That would be raw dictatorship. But few people with this propensity feel any pangs of conscience if it can be demonstrated that "the people voted for it." Thus, those who achieve political power are prone to seek popular sanction for their acts of legal plunder. And, as government increases its plundering activities, more and more citizens "want in" on the popular say-so. Thus, it is that pressures

---

[2] Responsibilities of citizenship involve a host of personal attributes, first and foremost a duty to one's Maker, duty to self, to family, to neighbors, and so on. Is it not evident, therefore, that voting is a mere formality after the fact? *It's much too late to be a responsible citizen if the responsibility hasn't been exercised before election day.* Everybody voted for Khrushchev in the last Russian election! Clearly, that was no evidence of responsible citizenship.

increase for the extension of the franchise. Time was when only property holders could vote or, perhaps, even cared to vote. Only in 1920 were women fully enfranchised. Now the drive is on to lower the age from 21 to 18, and this has already been achieved in some places.

Frederic Bastiat gave us some good thoughts on this subject:

> If law were restricted to protecting all persons, all liberties, and all properties; if law were nothing more than the organized combination of the individual's right to self-defense; if law were the obstacle, the check, the punisher of all oppressions and plunder—is it likely that we citizens would then argue much about the extent of the franchise?
>
> Under these circumstances, is it likely that the extent of the right to vote would endanger that supreme good, the public peace? Is it likely that the excluded classes would refuse to peaceably await the coming of their right to vote? Is it likely that those who had the right to vote would jealously defend their privilege?
>
> If the law were confined to its proper functions, everyone's interest in the law would be the same. Is it not clear that, under these circumstances, those who voted could not inconvenience those who did not vote?[3]

Selection by Lot

We can, it seems to me, glean from the foregoing that there is no moral or political or social obligation to vote merely because we are confronted with ballots having names and/or issues printed thereon. Is this so-called obligation of a citizen to vote, *regardless of the ballot presentations,* any more than a camouflage for political madness

---

[3] See *The Law* by Frederic Bastiat, pp. 16-17.

on the rampage? And, further, doesn't this "obligation" deny to the citizen the only alternative left to him—not to endorse persons or measures he regards as repugnant? When presented with two trimmers, how else, *at this level,* is he to protest? Abstinence from ballot-casting would appear to be his only way to avoid being untrue to himself.

If we seek more evidence than we now have as to the sacrosanctity of ballot casting as a citizenship duty, we need only observe the crusading spirit of get-out-the-vote campaigns. One is made to feel like a slacker if he does not respond.

To rob this get-out-the-vote myth of its glamour, no more is required than to compare ballot-casting as a means of selecting representatives with a method *devoid of all voter judgment:* selection by lot. Politically unthinkable as it is, reflect, just for fun, on your own congressional district. Disqualify those under 21, the insane, all illiterates, and all convicts.[4] Write the names of the balance on separate cards to put into a mixing machine, and let some blindfolded person withdraw one card. Presto! Here is your next representative in Congress, *for one term only.* After all, how can a person qualify to vote if he is not qualified to hold the office himself? And, further, it is assumed, he will feel duty-bound to serve, as when called for jury duty.

The first reaction to such a proposal is one of horror: "Why, we might get only an ordinary citizen." Compare such a prospect with one of two wrongdoers which all too

---

[4] One might like to disqualify everybody who receives government aid but, then, who would remain? The very bread we eat is subsidized. Those who ride on planes or use the mails, and so on, would be disqualified.

frequently is our only choice under a two-party, ballot-casting system that no longer presupposes any agreement on constitutional questions and the aims of government. Further, I submit that there is no governmental official today who can qualify as anything better than an "ordinary citizen." How can he possibly claim any superiority over those upon whose votes his election depends? And, it is of the utmost importance that we never ascribe anything more than "ordinary" to any of them. Not one among the millions in officialdom is in any degree omniscient, all-seeing, or competent in the slightest to rule over the creative aspects of any other citizen. The recognition that a citizen chosen by lot could be no more than an ordinary citizen would be all to the good. This would automatically strip officialdom of that aura of almightiness which so commonly attends it; government would be unseated from its master's role and restored to its servant's role, a highly desirable shift in emphasis.

Reflect on some of the other probable consequences:

a. With nearly everyone conscious that only "ordinary citizens" were occupying political positions, the question of *who should rule* would lose its significance. Immediately, we would become acutely aware of the far more important question: *What shall be the extent of the rule?* That we would press for a severe limitation of the state seems almost self-evident.

b. No more talk of a "third party" as a panacea. Political parties—now more or less meaningless—would cease to exist.

c. No more campaign speeches with their promises of how

much better we would fare were the candidates to spend our income for us.

d. An end to campaign fund-raising.

e. No more self-chosen "saviors" catering to base desires in order to win elections.

f. An end to that type of voting in Congress which has an eye more to re-election than to what's right.

g. The mere prospect of having to go to Congress during a lifetime, even though there would be but one chance in some 10,000, would completely reorient citizens' attention to the principles which bear on government's relationship to society. Everyone would have an incentive to "bone up," as the saying goes, if for no other reason than not to make a fool of himself, just in case! There would be an enormous increase in self-directed education in an area on which the future of society depends. In other words, the strong tendency would be to bring out the best, not the worst, in every citizen.

It would, of course, be absurd to work out the details, to refine, to suggest the scope of a selection-by-lot design, for it hardly falls within the realm of either probability or possibility—at least, not for a long, long time. Further, the real problem is at a depth not to be reached by merely meddling with the present machinery.

Why, if one believes selection by lot to be superior to the present degraded system, should one not urge immediate reform? Let me slightly rephrase an explanation by Gustave Le Bon:

The reason is that it is not within our power to force sudden transformations in complex social organisms. Nature has recourse, at times to radical measures, but never after our fashion, which explains how it is that nothing is more fatal to a people than the mania for great reforms, however excellent these reforms may appear theoretically. They would only be useful were it possible suddenly to change a whole nation of people. Institutions (social organisms) and laws are but the outward manifestation or outcome of the underlying ideas, sentiments, customs, in short, character. To urge a different outcome would in no way alter men's character—or the outcome.[5]

Why, then, should selection by lot be so much as mentioned? Merely to let the mind dwell on this intriguing alternative to current political inanities gives all the ammunition one needs to refrain from casting a ballot for one of two candidates, neither of whom is guided by integrity. Unless we can divorce ourselves from this unprincipled myth, we are condemned to a political competition that has only one end: the omnipotent state. This would conclude all economic freedom and with it freedom of speech, of the press, of worship. And even freedom to vote will be quite worthless—as it is under any dictatorship.

The problems of our times lie much deeper than the mechanics of selecting political representation; responsible citizenship demands, at the minimum, a personal attention to and a constant re-examination of one's own ideas, sentiments, customs. Such scrutiny may reveal that voting for candidates who bear false witness is not required of the good citizen. At the very least, the idea merits thoughtful exploration.

---

[5] See *The Crowd* by Gustave Le Bon (New York: The Viking Press, 1960), p. 4.

CHAPTER 10

ON KEEPING THE PEACE

MY THESIS, in simplest terms, is: Let anyone do anything he pleases, so long as it is peaceful; the role of government, then, is to keep the peace.

In suggesting that the function of government is only to keep the peace, I raise the whole issue between statists or socialists, on the one hand, and the devotees of the free market, private property, limited government philosophy on the other.

Keeping the peace means no more than prohibiting persons from unpeaceful actions. This, with its elaborate machinery for defining what shall be prohibited (codifying the law), along with the interpretation, administration, and enforcement of the law, is all the prohibition I want from government—for me or for anyone else. When government goes beyond this, that is, when government prohibits peaceful actions, such prohibitions themselves are, *prima facie,* unpeaceful. How much of a statist a person is can be judged by how far he would go in prohibiting peaceful actions.

The difference between the socialist and the student of liberty is a difference of opinion as to what others should be prohibited from doing. At least, we may use this as a working hypothesis, think it through, and test its validity. If the claim proves valid, then we have come upon a fairly simple method for distinguishing between warlike and peaceful persons—between authoritarians and libertarians.[1] But first, let us consider prohibitions in general.

How many animal species have come and gone no one knows. Many thousands survive and the fact of their existence, whether guided by instincts or drives or conscious choices, rests, in no small measure, on the avoidance of self-destructive actions. Thus, all surviving species have, at the very minimum, abided by a set of prohibitions—things not to do; otherwise, they would have been extinct ere this.

Certain types of scorpions, for example, stick to dry land; puddles and pools are among their instinctual taboos. There is some prohibitory force that keeps fish off dry land, lambs from chasing lions, and so on and on. How insects and animals acquire their built-in prohibitions is not well understood. We label their reactions instinctual, meaning that it is not reasoned or conscious behavior.

Man, on the other hand, does not now possess a like set of instinctual do-nots, prohibitions. Instead, he must en-

---

[1] Some will make the point that the authoritarian employs compulsions as well as prohibitions. My thesis is that all compulsions can be reduced to prohibitions, thus making it easier to assess authoritarianism. For instance, we say that a Russian is compelled to work in the sputnik factory. But it is more accurate to say that he is prohibited from any other employment; he builds sputniks or starves, and freely decides between the restricted choices left to him. So-called compulsions by government are, in fact, prohibitions of freedom to choose.

joy or suffer the consequences of his own free will, his own power to choose between right and wrong actions; in a word, man is more or less at the mercy of his own imperfect understanding and conscious decisions. The upshot of this is that human beings must choose the prohibitions they will observe, and the selection of a wrong one may be as disastrous to our species as omitting a right one. Survival of the human species rests as much on observing the correct prohibitions as is the case with any other species.

But in our case, the *observance* of the correct must-nots has survival value only if preceded by a correct, conscious *selection* of the must-nots. When the survival of the human race is at stake and when that survival rests on the selection of prohibitions by variable, imperfect members of that race, the wonder is that the ideological controversy is not greater than now.

When Homo sapiens first appeared he had little language, no literature, no maxims, no tradition or history to which he could make reference; in short, he possessed no precise and accurate list of things not to do. We cannot explain the survival of these early specimens of our kind unless we assume that some of the instinctual prohibitions of their earlier cousins remained with them during the transition period from instinct to some measure of self-knowledge; for, with respect to many millennia of that earlier period, we know nothing of man-formalized prohibitions. Then appeared the crude taboos observed by what we now call "primitive peoples." These had survival value under certain conditions, even though the reasons given for their practice might not hold water.

Three Forms of Persuasion

If prohibitions are as important as here represented, it is well that we reflect on the man-contrived thou-shalt-nots, particularly as to the several types of persuasiveness—for there can be no prohibition worth the mention unless it is backed by some form of persuasion. So far as this exploration is concerned, there are three forms of persuasion which make prohibitions effective or meaningful. I shall comment on the three forms in the order of their historical appearance.

The Code of Hammurabi, 2000 B.C., is probably the earliest of systematized prohibitions. This is considered one of the greatest of the ancient codes; it was particularly strong in its prohibitions against defrauding the helpless, that is, against unpeaceful actions directed at the helpless. To secure observance, the "persuasiveness" took the form of organized police force. *The Columbia Encyclopedia* refers to the retributive nature of the punishment meted out as a "savage feature . . . an eye for an eye literally." Not only is this the oldest of the three forms of persuasion employed to effectuate prohibitions and to keep the peace, but it remains to this day an important means of persuasion.

The next and higher form of persuasion appeared about a millennium later—the series of thou-shalt-nots known as The Decalogue. Here the backing was not organized police force but, instead, the promise of retribution: initially, the hope of tribal survival if the commands were obeyed, and the fear of tribal extinction were they disobeyed, and, later, the hope of heavenly bliss or the fear of hell and damnation. It may be said that The Decalogue exemplifies moral rather than political law and, also, that its form of persuasion advanced from physical force to a type of spiritual influence. We witness in this evolutionary step the emergence of man's moral nature.

The latest and highest form of persuasion is that which gives effectiveness to the most advanced prohibition, The Golden Rule. As originally scribed, around 500 B.C., it read: "Do not do unto others that which you would not have them do unto you." What persuasiveness lies behind it? Not physical force. And not even such spiritual influences as hope and fear. Force and influence give way to a desire for righteousness: *a sense of justice,* regarded as the inmost law of one's being. That this is a recently acquired faculty is attested to by its rarity. Ever so many people will concede the soundness of the prohibition, but only now and then do we find an individual whose moral nature is elevated to the point where he can observe this moral imperative in daily living. The individual with an elevated moral nature has moved beyond the concept of external rewards and punishments to the conviction that virtue and excellence are their own reward.

An Elevated Moral Nature

It is relevant to that which follows to reflect on what is meant by an elevated moral nature. To illustrate the lack of such a nature: We had a kitchen employee who pilfered, that is, she would quietly lift provisions from our larder and tote them home to her own. This practice did no offense to such moral scruples as she possessed; she was only concerned lest anyone see her indulge it; nothing was wrong except getting caught! My point is that this individual had not yet acquired what is here meant by an elevated moral nature.

What is to distinguish the individual who has an elevated moral nature? For one thing, he cares not one whit about what others see him do. Why? He has a private eye of his own, far more exacting and severe than any force or influence others can impose: a highly developed conscience. Not only does such a person possess a sense of justice but he also possesses its counterpart, a disciplinary conscience. Justice and conscience are two parts of the same emerging moral faculty. It is doubtful that one part can exist without the other.

It seems that individual man, having lost many of the built-in, instinctual do-nots of his earlier cousins, acquires, as he evolves far enough, a built-in, rational, prohibitory ethic which he is compelled to observe by reason of his sense of justice and the dictates of his conscience. We repeat, proper prohibitions are just as important to the survival of the human species as to the survival of any other species.

Do not do to others that which you would not have them do unto you. There is more to this prohibition than first glance reveals. Nearly everyone, for instance, will concede that there is no universal right to kill, to steal, or to enslave—that such behavior could never be tolerated as a general practice. But only the person who comprehends this ethic in its wholeness, who has an elevated sense of justice and conscience, will see clearly why this denies to him the right to take the life of another, to relieve any person of his livelihood, or to deprive any human being of his liberty. And, one more distinction: While there are many who will agree that they, personally, should not kill, steal, enslave, it is only the individual with an elevated moral nature who will have no hand in encouraging any agency—even government—to do these things on behalf of himself or others. He clearly sees that the popular expedient of collective action affords no escape from individual responsibility.

What Shall Be Prohibited?

Let us now return to the question this essay poses: "What shall be prohibited?" For it is the difference of opinion as to what should be denied others that highlights the essential difference between the collectivists—socialists, statists, interventionists, mercantilists, disturbers of the peace—and those of the peaceful, libertarian faith. Take stock of what you would prohibit others from doing and you will accurately find your own position in the ideological line-up. This method can be used to determine anyone's position.

The following statement came to my attention as I was writing this chapter:

> Government has a positive responsibility in any just society to see to it that each and every one of its citizens acquires all the skills and all the opportunities necessary to practice and appreciate the arts to the limit of his natural ability. Enjoyment of the arts and participation in them are among

man's natural rights and essential to his full development as
a civilized person. One of the reasons governments are insti-
tuted among men is to make this right a reality.[2]

It is significant that the author uses the term "its citizens," the antecedent being government. Such a concep-
tion is basic to the collectivistic philosophy: *We*—you and
I—*belong* to the state. Of course, if one accepts this statist
premise—this wholesale invasion of peaceful actions—the
above quote is sensible enough: it has to do with a detail
in the state's paternalistic concern for us as its wards.

But we are on another tack, namely, examining what a
person would prohibit others from doing. The author just
quoted suggests no prohibitions, at least, not to anyone who
fails to read below the surface. He dwells only on what he
would have the state do *for* the people. Where, then, are
the prohibitions? The "civilized" program he favors would
cost X million dollars annually. From where come these
millions? The state has nothing except that which it takes
from the people. Therefore, this man favors that we, the
people, be prohibited from peacefully using the fruits of
our own labor as we choose in order that these fruits be
expended as the state chooses. And take note that this and
all other socialist-designed prohibitions of peaceful pursuits have police force as the method of persuasion.

To repeat what was stated in a previous chapter, socialism has a double-barreled definition, one of which is the
state ownership and/or control of the *results* of production. Our incomes are the results of production. That portion of our incomes is socialized which the state turns to

---

[2] See *The Commonweal*, August 23, 1963, p. 494.

its use rather than our own. It follows, then, that a person would impose prohibitions on the rest of us to the extent that he supports governmental projects such as forcibly taking the fruits of our labor to assure others an "enjoyment of the arts."

Only a few, as yet, favor the socialization of the arts and the consequent socialization of our incomes, but there are ever so many who favor prohibiting our freedom peacefully to use the fruits of our own labor in order to:

—perform our charities for us;

—protect us from floods, droughts, hurricanes, earthquakes, fires, freezes, insects, and other hazards;

—insure us against illness, accident, old age;

—subsidize below-cost pricing in air, water, and land transportation, education, insurance, loans of countless kinds;

—put three men on the moon (estimated at $40,000,000,-000) ;

—give federal aid of this or that variety, endlessly.

This is the welfare state side of socialism.

The above, however, does not exhaust the prohibitions that the socialists would impose on our peaceful actions. For socialism, also, is the state ownership and/or control of the *means* of production. We are now prohibited from:

—freely planting our own acreage to wheat, cotton, peanuts, corn, tobacco, rice, even if used only to feed our own stock;

—quitting our own business at will;

—taking a job at will;

—pricing our own services (wages) ;

—delivering first-class mail for pay;

—selling our own product at our own price, for instance, milk, steel, and so on.

—free entry into business activities, like producing power and light in the Tennessee Valley.

This is the planned economy side of socialism.

Again, the listing of prohibitions is endless. Harold Fleming, author of *Ten Thousand Commandments* (1951), having to do with prohibitions of just one federal agency —The Federal Trade Commission—claims that the book, if brought up-to-date, would be titled, *Twenty Thousand Commandments*.

Those who favor the socialization of the *means* of production would, of course, prohibit profit and even deny the validity of the profit motive.

Preserving the Peace

Of all the prohibitions listed above plus others that are implicit in socialism, which do you or others favor? This is the appropriate question for rating oneself or others ideologically.

Persons devoted to liberty would, it is true, impose certain prohibitions on others. They merely note that not all individuals have acquired sufficient moral stature strictly to observe such moral laws as "Thou shalt not kill" and "Thou shalt not steal." There are in the population those who will take the lives and the livelihood of others, those who will pilfer and those who will get the government to do their pilfering for them. Most libertarians would supplement the moral laws aimed at prohibiting violence to another's person (life) or another's livelihood (extension of life).[3] Thus they would prohibit or at least penalize murder, theft, fraud, misrepresentation. In short, they would inhibit or prohibit the *destructive or unpeaceful* actions of any and all! Says the student of liberty, "Freely choose how you act creatively, productively, peacefully. I have no desire to prohibit you or others in this respect. I have no prohibitory designs on you of any kind except as you would unpeacefully keep me and others from acting creatively, productively, peacefully, as we freely choose."

Be it noted that the libertarian in his hoped-for prohibition of unpeaceful actions does not have in mind any violence to anyone else's liberty, none whatsoever. For this reason: The word liberty would never be used by an individual completely isolated from others; it is a social term. We must not, therefore, think of liberty as being restrained when fraud, violence, and the like are prohibited, for such actions violate the liberty of others, and liberty cannot be composed of liberty negations. This is self-evident. Thus, any accomplished student of liberty would never prohibit the liberty or the peaceful actions of another.

There we have it: the socialists with the countless prohibitions of liberty they would impose on others; the students of liberty whose suggested prohibitions are not opposed to but are in support of liberty and are as few and

---

[3] How prohibited? Unfortunately, by physical force or the threat thereof, the only form of persuasion comprehensible to those lacking a developed sense of morality and justice. Be it noted, however, that this is exclusively a *defensive* force, called into play only as a secondary action, that is, it is inactive except in the instances of initiated, *aggressive* force.

as simple as the two Commandments against the taking of life and livelihood. Interestingly enough, it is the socialists, the all-out prohibitionists, who call nonintervening, peaceful libertarians "extremists." Their nomenclature leaves as much to be desired as does their theory of political economy!

But the students of liberty and the socialists have one position in common: the human situation is not in apple pie order; imperfection is rampant. The student of liberty, however, observing that human imperfection is universal, balks at halting the evolutionary process, such halting being the ultimate prohibition implicit in all authoritarian schemes. Be the political dandy a Napoleon or Tito or one of the home grown variety of prohibitionists, how can the human situation improve if the rest of us are not permitted to grow beyond the level of the political dandy's imperfections? Is nothing better in store for humanity than this?

The libertarian's answer is affirmative: There *is* something better! But the improvement must take the form of man's growth, emergence, hatching—the acquisition of higher faculties such as an improved sense of justice, a refined, exacting, self-disciplinary conscience, in brief, an elevated moral nature. Man-concocted prohibitions against this growth stifle or kill it. Human faculties can flower, man can move toward his creative destiny, only if he be free to do so, in a word, where peace and liberty prevail.

What should be prohibited? *Actions which impair liberty and peace!*

CHAPTER 11

ONLY GOD CAN MAKE A TREE— OR A PENCIL

As I sat contemplating the miraculous make-up of an ordinary lead pencil, the thought flashed in mind: I'll bet there isn't a person on earth who knows how to make even so simple a thing as a pencil. If this could be demonstrated, it would dramatically portray the miracle of the market and would help to make clear that all manufactured things are but manifestations of creative energy exchanges; that these are, in fact, spiritual phenomena. The lessons in political economy this could teach!

There followed that not-to-be forgotten day at the pencil factory, beginning at the receiving dock; covering every phase of countless transformations, and concluding in an interview with the chemist.

Had you seen what I saw, you, also, might have struck up a warm friendship with that amazing character, I, PENCIL.[1] Being a writer in his own right, let I, PENCIL speak for himself:

---

[1] His official name is "Mongol 482." His many ingredients are assembled, fabricated, and finished by Eberhard Faber Pencil Company, Wilkes-Barre, Pennsylvania.

136

I AM a lead pencil—the ordinary wooden pencil familiar to all boys and girls and adults who can read and write.

Writing is both my vocation and my avocation; that's all I do.

You may wonder why I should write this genealogy. Well, to begin with, my story is fascinating. I am a mystery —more so than a tree or a sunset or even a flash of lightning. But sad to say, I am, like all abundant things, taken for granted by those who use me, as if I were a mere incident and without background. This supercilious attitude relegates me to the level of the commonplace. This is a grievous error in which mankind cannot too long persist without peril. For, as a wise man observed, "We are perishing for want of wonder, not for want of wonders."[2]

I, Pencil, simple though I appear to be, merit your wonder and awe, a claim I shall attempt to prove. In fact, if you can understand me—no, that's too much to ask of anyone— if you can become aware of the miraculousness which I symbolize, you can help save the freedom mankind is so unhappily losing. I have a profound lesson to teach. And I can teach this lesson better than can an automobile or a jet plane or a mechanical dishwasher because—well, because I am seemingly so simple.

Simple? Yet, *not a single person on the face of this earth knows how to make me!* This sounds fantastic doesn't it? Especially when it is realized that there are more than one and one-half billion of my kind manufactured in the U.S.A. annually.

---

[2] G. K. Chesterton.

Pick me up and look me over. What do you see? Not much meets the eye—there's some wood, lacquer, the printed labeling, the lead, a bit of metal, and an eraser.

Just as you cannot trace your family tree back very far, so is it impossible for me to name and explain all my antecedents. But I would like to suggest enough of them to impress upon you the richness and complexity of my background.

The Raw Materials

My family tree begins with what in fact is a tree, a cedar of straight grain that grows in Northern California and Oregon. Now contemplate all the saws and trucks and rope and the countless other gear used in harvesting and carting the cedar logs to the railroad siding. Think of all the persons and their numberless skills that went into the fabrication: the mining of ore, the making of steel and its refinement into saws, axes, motors; the growing of hemp and bringing it through all the stages to heavy and strong rope; the logging camps with their beds and mess halls, the cookery and the raising of all the foods. Why, untold thousands of persons had a hand in every cup of coffee the loggers drink!

The logs are shipped to a mill in San Leandro, California. Can you imagine the individuals who make flat cars and rails and railroad engines and who construct and install the communication systems incidental thereto? These legions are among my antecedents.

Consider the millwork in San Leandro. The cedar logs are cut into small, pencil-length slats less than one-fourth of an inch in thickness. These are kiln dried and then tinted for the same reason women put rouge on their faces. People prefer that I look pretty, not a pallid white. The slats are waxed and kiln dried again. How many skills went into the making of the tint and the kilns, into supplying the heat, the light and power, the belts, motors, and all the other things a mill requires? Sweepers in the mill among my ancestors? Yes, and included are the men who poured the concrete for the dam of a Pacific Gas & Electric Company hydroplant which supplies the mill's power.

Don't overlook the ancestors present and distant who have a hand in transporting sixty carloads of slats across the nation from California to Wilkes-Barre!

Once in the pencil factory—$4,000,000 in machinery and building, all capital accumulated by thrifty and saving parents of mine—each slat is given eight grooves by a complex machine. Then a second machine lays leads in every other slat, applies glue, and places another slat atop—a lead sandwich, so to speak. Seven brothers and I are mechanically carved from this "wood-clinched" sandwich.

My "lead" itself—it contains no lead at all—is complex. The graphite is mined in Ceylon. Consider these miners and those who make their many tools and the makers of the paper sacks in which the graphite is shipped and those who make the string that ties the sacks and those who put them aboard ships and those who make the ships. Even the lighthouse keepers along the way assisted in my birth—and the harbor pilots.

The graphite is mixed with clay from Mississippi, with ammonium hydroxide used in the refining process. Then wetting agents are added such as sulfonated tallow—animal fats chemically reacted with sulfuric acid. After passing through numerous machines, the mixture finally appears in endless extrusions—as from a sausage grinder—cut to size, dried, and baked for several hours at 1,850 degrees Fahrenheit. To increase their strength and smoothness the leads are than treated with a hot mixture which includes candelilla wax from Mexico, paraffin wax, and hydrogenated natural fats.

My cedar receives six coats of lacquer. Do you know all of the ingredients of lacquer? Who would think that the growers of castor beans and the refiners of castor oil are a part of it? They are! Why, even the processes by which the lacquer is made a beautiful yellow involve the skills of more persons than one can enumerate!

Observe the labeling. That's a film formed by applying heat to carbon black mixed with resins. How do you make resins and what, pray, is carbon black?

My bit of metal—the ferrule—is brass. Think of all the persons who mine zinc and copper and those who have the skills to make shiny sheet brass from these products of nature. Those black rings on my ferrule are black nickel. What is black nickel and how is it applied? The complete story of why the center of my ferrule has no black nickel on it would take pages to explain.

Then there's my crowning glory, inelegantly referred to in the trade as "the plug," the part man uses to erase the errors he makes with me. An ingredient called "factice" is what does the erasing. It is a rubber-like product made by reacting rape seed oil from Sweden with sulfur chloride. Rubber, contrary to the common notion, is only for binding purposes. Then, too, there are numerous vulcanizing and accelerating agents. The pumice comes from Italy; and the pigment which gives "the plug" its color is cadmium sulfide.

No One Knows It All

Does anyone wish to challenge my earlier assertion that no single person on the face of the earth knows how to make me?

Actually, millions of human beings have had a hand in my creation, no one of whom knows more than a very few of the others. Now, you may say that I go too far in relating the picker of a coffee berry in far off Brazil and food growers elsewhere to my creation; that this is an extreme position. I shall stand by my claim. There isn't a single person in all these millions, including the president of the pencil company, who contributes more than a tiny, infinitesimal bit of know-how. From the standpoint of know-how, the only difference between the miner of graphite in Ceylon and the logger in Oregon is in the *type* of know-how. Neither the miner nor the logger can be dispensed with, any more than can the chemist at the factory or the worker in the oil field —paraffin being a by-product of petroleum.

Here is an astounding fact: Neither the worker in the oil field nor the chemist nor the digger of graphite or clay nor any who mans or makes the ships or trains or trucks nor the one who runs the machine that does the knurling on my bit of metal nor the president of the company performs his singular task because he wants me. Each one wants me less, perhaps, than does a child in the first grade. Indeed, there are some among this vast multitude who never saw a pencil nor would they know how to use one. Their motivation is other than me. Perhaps it is something like this: Each of these millions sees that he can thus exchange his tiny know-how for the goods and services he needs or wants. I may or may not be among these items.

There is a fact still more astounding: the absence of a master mind, of anyone dictating or forcibly directing these countless actions which bring me into being. No trace of such a person can be found. Instead, we find the Invisible Hand at work. This is the mystery to which I earlier referred.

"Only God Can Make a Tree"

A poet has said that "only God can make a tree." Why do we agree with this? Isn't it because we realize that we ourselves could not make one? Indeed, can we even describe a tree? We cannot, except in superficial terms. We can say, for instance, that a certain molecular configuration manifests itself as a tree. But what mind is there among men that could even record, let alone direct, the constant changes in molecular arrangements that transpire in the life span of a tree? Such a feat is utterly unthinkable!

I, Pencil, am a complex combination of miracles: a tree, zinc, copper, graphite, and so on. But to these miracles which manifest themselves in Nature an even more extraordinary miracle has been added: the configuration of creative human energies—millions of tiny know-hows configurating naturally and spontaneously in response to human necessity and desire and *in the absence of any human master-minding*.

Since only God can make a tree, I insist that only God could make me. Man can no more direct these millions of know-hows to bring me into being than he can put molecules together to create a tree.

The above is what I meant when writing, "If you can become aware of the miraculousness which I symbolize, you can help save the freedom mankind is so unhappily losing." For, if one is aware that these know-hows will naturally, yes, automatically arrange themselves into creative and productive patterns in response to human necessity and demand—that is, in the absence of governmental or any other coercive master-minding—then one will possess an absolutely essential ingredient for freedom: *a faith in free men.* Freedom is impossible without this faith. Why? Without this faith there is nothing to believe in except controlled men. It's either a faith in free men and peace—or the lack of it and violence. There is no third alternative.

The lesson I have to teach is this: Leave all creative energies uninhibited, and thus make it possible for people to organize themselves in harmony with this lesson. Let society's legal apparatus remove all obstacles as best it can, that is, let it keep the peace. Merely permit these creative know-hows freely to flow. Have faith in what free men will accomplish. Not only will this faith be confirmed but it has been and is confirmed to us daily, in evidence so abundant that we seldom take notice of it. I, Pencil, seemingly simple though I am, offer the miracle of my creation as testimony that faith in free men is a practical faith, as practical as the sun, the rain, a cedar tree, the good earth.

CHAPTER 12

THE MOST IMPORTANT
DISCOVERY IN ECONOMICS

THE SOCIALISTIC or governmentally planned system pre-supposes bureaucrats competent to control the actions of others. The market economy, by contrast, rests on the free exchange of goods and services among ordinary citizens; it doesn't depend on supermen, not even one!

The Bible informs us that "the meek shall inherit the earth." Quite obviously, "the meek" had no reference to the Mr. Milquetoasts in society but, rather, to *the teachable*. The teachable—those who aspire to an ever greater under-standing—are those with an awareness of how little they know. Lest teachableness and inferiority be associated, consider a more likely correlation: teachableness and wis-dom. Said Socrates, "This man thinks he knows some-thing when he does not, whereas I, as I do not know anything, do not think I do either." For such acknowledg-ments of fallibility, Socrates was acclaimed a wise man. He and many others—for instance, Lecomte du Noüy and Robert Milliken, scientists of our time—discovered, as they expanded their own consciousness, that they progressively exposed themselves to more and more of the unknown. Edison's fact-packed, inquiring, ever-curious mind concluded, "we don't know a millionth of one per cent about anything. We are just emerging from the chimpanzee state." These teachable persons came to realize how little they knew; and that, perhaps, is a measure of wisdom.

For the student of liberty and of economics, this poses an interesting question: Is it possible to have a workable, productive economy premised on a society of teachable individuals—those who know very little and know they know very little?

We can assume that such an economy would differ markedly from a society planned by those who have no question about their omniscience, those at the other end of the intellectual spectrum who see no difficulty at all in their design for arranging the lives of everyone else. Like the group of seven economists who voiced this authoritarian and unpeaceful view: "The Federal government is our only instrument for guiding the economic destiny of the country."[1]

The federal government, in such a role, must be staffed largely with those who are unaware of how little they know, who have no qualms about their ability to plan and regulate the national economic growth, set wages, prescribe hours of work, write the price tags for everything, decide how much of what shall be produced, expand or contract the money supply arbitrarily, set interest rates and rents, subsidize with other peoples' earnings whatever activity strikes their fancy, lend billions not voluntarily entrusted to them, allocate the fruits of the labor of all to foreign

---

[1] Quoted in *First National City Bank Letter,* August, 1959, p. 90.

governments of their choice—in short, decide what shall be taken from each Peter and how much of the "take" shall be paid to each Paul.

Government control and ownership of the means and/or the results of production is authoritarianism, be it called state interventionism, socialism, or communism. It rests on the premise that certain persons possess the intelligence to understand and guide all human action. It is advocated by those who sense no lack of omniscience in themselves, by the naive followers of such egotists, by the seekers of power over others, by those who foresee an advantage to themselves in these political manipulations, and by those "do-gooders" who fail to distinguish between police grants-in-aid and the Judeo-Christian principles of charity. All in all, they are a considerable number, but still a minority in terms of the tens of millions whose lives they would regulate.

The most important point to bear in mind is that socialism presupposes that government or officialdom is the endower, dispenser, and the source of men's rights, as well as the guide, controller, and director of their energies. This is the Supremacy of Egotism: The State is God; *we* are the State!

The Egotist Examined

Let us then examine a typical egotist. It matters not whom you choose—a professor, a professional politician, a Napoleon, a Hitler, a Stalin—but the more pretentious the better. (As H. G. Wells put it, "A high-brow is a low-brow plus pretentiousness.") Simply admit some supreme egotist into your mind's eye and take stock of him. Study his private life. You will usually discover that his wife, his children, his neighbors, those in his hire, fail to respond to his dictates in ways he thinks proper.[2] This is to say, the egotist is frequently a failure in the very situations nearest and best known to him. Incongruously, he then concludes that he is called to manage whole societies—or even the world! Fie on anything small enough to occupy an ordinary man!

Let's further test the knowledge of the egotist. He wants to plan production; what does he know about it? Here, for example, is a company in the U.S.A. which manufactures well over 200,000 separate items. Not one person in the company knows what these items are, and there is no individual on the face of the earth, as I have demonstrated,[3] who has the skills, by himself, to make a single one of them. It's a safe bet that the egotist under scrutiny has never been closer to this company than a textbook description of corporations in general by fellow egotists. Yet, he would put this intricate mechanism under the rigid control of government and would have no hesitancy at all in accepting the post of Chief Administrator. He would then arbitrarily allocate and price all raw materials and manpower and, after long and complicated statistics of the past, arbitrarily allocate and price the more than 200,000

---

[2] Napoleon's domestic affairs were a mess and his numerous family drove him to distraction; Hitler was an indifferent paper hanger; Stalin tried first theology and then train robbery before he elected bureaucracy and dictatorship; many bureaucrats charged with great affairs have no record of personal success.

[3] See Chapter 11.

finished products, most of which he never knew existed. Involved in the operations of this company alone—a mere fraction of the American economy—are incalculable human energy exchanges, but the egotist would manage these with a few "big man" gestures! Such cursory attention he would find necessary for, bear in mind, he also would have under his control the lives, livelihoods, and activities of nearly two hundred million individuals not directly associated with this company.

Next, what does the egotist know about exchange? In a specialized or division-of-labor economy like ours, exchange cannot be carried on by primitive barter. It is accomplished by countless interchanges interacting on one another with the aid of a generally accepted medium of exchange. The socialistic philosophy of the egotists presupposes that there are persons competent to regulate and control the volume and value of money and credit. Yet, surely no one person or committee is any more competent to manipulate the supply of money and credit to attain a definite end than he or a committee is able to make an automobile or a lead pencil!

An economy founded on nonexistent know-it-allness is patently absurd!

But, can there be a sensible rational economy founded on the premise of know-next-to-nothingness? An economy that would run rings around socialism? In short, is there a highly productive way of life which presupposes no human prescience, no infallibility, nothing beyond an awareness that it is simply not man's to pattern others in his own image? *There is such a way!*

For the Teachable

Contrary to socialism, this way of life is for teachable people who concede their fallibility—and it denies that government, staffed by fallible people, is the source of men's rights. It holds, as developed earlier, that rights to life, livelihood, and liberty are endowments of the Creator and that the purpose of government is to secure these rights. When Creativity is assumed to exist over and beyond the conscious mind of man, a whole new concept of man's relationship to man emerges. Man, once he conceives of himself in this setting, knows that he is not really knowledgeable but is, at best, only teachable. The greatest conscious fact of his life is his awareness of the Unknown.

To illustrate, let us observe how such a person "builds" his own house. He does not think of himself as actually having built it. No man living could do that. He thinks of himself as having done only an assembly job. He is aware of numerous preconditions, two of which are:

1. The provisioning of his materials done exclusively by others, the unbelievable complexity of which I tried to explain in the previous chapter.

2. A reasonable absence of destructive or unpeaceful actions. No thieves stole his supplies. His suppliers had not defrauded him nor had they misrepresented their wares. Violence, like coercively keeping others from working where they freely chose (strikes) or like coercively keeping others from freely exchanging the products of their labor (protectionism) had not succeeded in denying these services to him. In short, interferences with creative, peaceful efforts and exchanges had not reached the point where a house was impossible.

The teachable man, the one who knows how little he knows, is aware that creative energies, and creative energy exchanges, work miracles if unhampered. The evidence is all about him. There are his automobile, the coffee he drinks, the meat he eats, the clothes he wears, the symphony he hears, the books he reads, the paintings he enjoys, the velvet he touches and, above all, the insights or inspiration or ideas that come to him—from where he does not know.

The teachable person looks with awe upon all creation.[4] He agrees that "only God can make a tree." And he also understands that, in the final analysis, only God can build a house. Nature, Creation, God—use your own term—if not interfered with, will combine atoms into molecules which, in a certain configuration, will form a tree, in another a blade of grass, in still another a rose—mysteries upon mysteries! And, there are demonstrations readily apparent to the teachable person that the creative energies of men, when not interfered with, configurate through space and time—and in response to human necessity and aspiration —to form houses, symphonies, food, clothes, airplanes . . . manufactured things in endless profusion.

The teachable person is likely to be aware of some wonderful cosmic force at work—a drawing, attracting, magnetic power—attending to perpetual creation. He may well conceive of himself as an agent through whom this power has the potentiality of flowing and, to the extent this occurs, to that degree does he have an opportunity to share

---

4 "If I may coin a new English word to translate a much nicer old Greek word, 'wanting-to-know-it-ness' was their characteristic; wonder . . . was the mother of their philosophy." *The Challenge of the Greek*, by T. R. Glover (New York: The Macmillan Company, 1942), pp. 6-7.

in the processes of creation. As agent, his psychological problem is to rid himself of his own inhibitory influences —fear, superstition, anger, and the like—in order that this power may freely flow. He knows that he cannot dictate to it, direct it, or even get results by commanding, "Now I shall create a symphony" or "Now I shall discover a cure for the common cold" or "Now I shall invent a way of impressing upon others how little they know." He is quite certain that he must not thwart this power as it pertains to his own personal being.

Let Energy Flow Freely

Society-wise, the teachable human being, the one who conceives of himself as agent through whom this mysterious, creative power has the potentiality of flowing, concedes that what applies to him must, perforce, apply to other human beings; that this same power has the potentiality of flowing through them; that his own existence, livelihood, and opportunity to serve as an agency of that power *depends* on how well these others fare creatively. He realizes that he can no more dictate its flow in others than in himself. He knows only that he must not thwart it in others and that it is to his interest and theirs, and to the interest of all society, that there be no thwarting of this force in anyone. Leave this power alone and let it work its miracles!

Creative action cannot be induced by any form of authoritarianism, be the commands directed at oneself or at others. However, any idiot can thwart these actions in himself or in others precisely as he can thwart the forces of creation from manifesting themselves as a tree. He can prevent a tree from being, but he cannot make it be. Coercive force can only inhibit, restrain, penalize, destroy. It cannot create!

The teachable individual, being peaceful, imposes no inhibitions, restraints, or penalties on creative actions. He leaves them free to wend their miraculous courses.

The man who knows how little he knows would like to see the removal of all destructive obstacles to the flow of creative energy and energy exchanges. But, even this, he doesn't quite know how to accomplish. He would rely mostly on an improved understanding of the Golden Rule, the Ten Commandments, and other consistent ethical and moral principles. He hopes that more and more persons eventually will see that even their own self-interest is never served by impairing the creative actions of others, or living off them as parasites.

In summary, then, the teachable person is content to leave creative energies and their exchanges untouched; and he would rely primarily on ethical precepts and practices to keep these energy circuits free of destructive invasion. The governmental apparatus would merely assist these precepts and practices by defending the lives and property of all citizens equally; by protecting all willing exchanges and restraining all unwilling exchanges; by suppressing and penalizing all fraud, all misrepresentation, all violence, all predatory practices; by invoking a common justice under written law; in short, by keeping the peace!

Very well. So far, in theory, creative energies or actions

and their exchanges are left unhampered. Destructive actions are self-disciplined or, if not, are restrained by the societal agency of law and defensive force. Is that all? Does not the person who is aware of how little he knows have to know a lot of economics?

How Much Must Be Known?

The man mentioned previously, who "built" his own house, has about as much economic understanding as is necessary. He reflects on all the countless antecedent services which he assembled into a finished home. Originally, all of these items came from Nature. They were there when the Indians foraged this same territory. There was no price on them in their raw state—they were for free, so to speak. Yet, he paid—let us say—$10,000 for them.

What was the payment for? Well, when we slice through all the economic terms, he paid for the human action that necessarily had to be applied to things of the good earth. He paid for actions and energies which he himself did not possess, or, possessing, did not choose to exert. Were he limited to his own energies to bring about the services antecedent to his assembly of them, he could not have built such a home in a thousand lifetimes.

These human actions for which he paid took several forms. Generalizing, his $10,000 covered salaries and wages that had been paid for judgment, foresight, skill, initiative, enterprise, research, management, invention, physical exertion, chance discovery, know-how; interest that had been paid for self-denial or waiting; dividends that had been paid for risking; rent that had been paid for locational advantage—in short, all of the $10,000 covered payments for one or another form of human action. Literally millions of individuals had a hand in the process.

The major economic problem—the root of economic hassles—reduced to its simplest terms, revolves around the question of who is going to get how much of that $10,000. How is economic justice to be determined? What part shall go to the grower of soybeans, to the investor in a saw mill, to the man who tends the machine that pours nails into wooden kegs, to the inventor of the machine, to the owner of the paint plant? *Who or what shall determine the answers?* This is the economic question of questions.

The Market Knows Best

How much economics does one have to know to settle, in one's own mind, how and by whom economic justice shall be rendered? He has to know and fully comprehend only this: *Let the payment for each individual's contribution be determined by what others will offer in willing exchange.* That's enough of economics for those who know they know not.[5]

This simple theory of value, the greatest discovery in economic science—never formalized until the year 1870—is known as the marginal utility theory of value. It also

---

[5] There are some who will contend that one must understand money, the medium of exchange. This, also, is an impossible requirement. For extended comments on this point of view, see my *Government: An Ideal Concept* (Irvington-on-Hudson, N. Y.: Foundation for Economic Education, Inc., 1954), pp. 80-91.

goes by two other names: "the subjective theory of value" and "the free market theory of value." Testimony to its simplicity was given by Eugen von Böhm-Bawerk, perhaps its greatest theoretician:

> And so the intellectual labor that people have to perform in estimating subjective value is not so astounding as may appear . . . incidentally, even if it were a considerably greater task than it actually is, one could still confidently entrust it to "John Doe and Richard Roe." . . . For centuries, long before science set up the doctrine of marginal utility, the common man was accustomed to seek things and abandon things . . . he practiced the doctrine of marginal utility before economic theory discovered it.[6]

The labor theory of value held scholarly sway prior to this free market theory. It contended that value was determined by the amount of effort expended or fatigue incurred. For example, some persons make mud pies, others mince pies. The same effort, let us assume, is expended in the preparation of each. Under the labor theory of value the mud pie makers should receive the same return for their efforts as the mince pie makers. The only way to accomplish this—consumers being unwilling to exchange the fruits of their labor for mud pies—is for the government to subsidize the mud pie makers by taking from the mince pie makers. Karl Marx elaborated upon and helped systematize this theory—governments taking from the productive and subsidizing the less productive.

---

[6] From pages 203-4, Vol. II, *Capital and Interest* by Eugen von Böhm-Bawerk (South Holland, Illinois: The Libertarian Press, 1959). This volume may be the best treatise on the marginal utility theory of value extant.

The labor theory of value, proved over and over again to be the enemy of both justice and sound economics, nonetheless continues to gain in popular acceptance. Emotional reactions to effort expended and fatigue incurred do not readily give way to reason. Sentimental thoughts such as "the poor, hard-working farmers" set the political stage for agricultural subsidies. Similarly, sympathies which emanate from such outmoded and erroneous reflections as "the down-trodden laboring man" condition most people to accept the coercive powers allowed labor unions.

Practice of the labor theory of value is rationalized by spenders, inflationists, Keynesians, egotists, on the ground that it puts purchasing power in the hands of those who will spend it. As set forth earlier, this man-concocted system of forcibly controlling creative human action—interventionism, socialism, communism—presupposes all-knowing bureaucrats; but, to date, not a single one has been found—not even a reasonable facsimile thereof.

The free market, on the other hand, is for the teachable, who know their own limitations, who feel no compulsions to play God, and who put their faith in voluntary, willing exchange—a manner of human relationships that miraculously works economic wonders for all without requiring infallibility of anyone.

CHAPTER 13

THE GREATEST COMPUTER
ON EARTH

WHEN A PERSON does not know how little he knows, he may try to change a room's temperature by monkeying with the thermometer; or, equally absurd, he may tamper with prices to control the market.

Wherever there are people, there will be a market of some sort. The market can no more be eliminated than can its primary components—production and exchange.

Further, the market, be it rigged or free, is an enormously complex computer. It receives the data fed into it and gives off signals in the form of prices. Keep in mind, however, that a computer cannot exercise judgment; its answers merely reflect the data it receives; feed it wrong data and its pricing signals will be misleading or, as they say in the computer profession, "GIGO!": *Garbage In, Garbage Out.*[1]

Consider, first, the free market computer, as if it really existed. Billions of data flow into it continuously. The data are composed of every wish, desire, fancy, whim, like, and dislike of every person on earth. Included in the data are all efficiencies, inefficiencies, inventions, discoveries, as well

---

[1] The pros pronounce it guy-go.

as the reports of all rising and falling supplies and demands. All degrees and variations of competitive forces and all bidding and asking prices of all goods and services are grist for the mill. Even people's anticipation of how a flood or a drought or a freeze might modify supply are automatically admitted, as are expectations of managerial competence or failure or the effects of a President's ideas or the state of his health or whatever.

The Ideal Free Market

The free market computer gives accurate answers in prices, signaling to all would-be entrepreneurs to get into production or get out, to step up or diminish particular economic activities. Supply and demand thus tend, automatically, toward equilibrium. The free market computer is truly free: its accurately instructive answers are founded on *free* exchange data; its services are *free,* with no more cost than the sun's energy; it *frees* each and all of us from the impossible task of assembling the billions upon billions of data behind our daily decisions.

The free market computer has never been permitted to function on a world-wide basis. It has had only partial, regional, short-run trials. Certainly, one of the most comprehensive tests occurred in the U.S.A. during the century beginning about 1830. Perhaps the small Crown Colony of Hong Kong affords the best test at this moment in history. We do know from a study of the evidence, as well as from *a priori* reasoning, that the less the free market computer is interfered with or "rigged" the better do people prosper, the more nearly universal is economic well-being.

The term GIGO is never applicable to the free market computer; the complex data are truthful, unrigged expressions of the universal economic situation in its continuous ebb and flow, and the price signals, ever changing, are accurate responses thereto.

The U.S.A. Market

Consider, second, something quite different, the U.S.A. market computer as it presently exists. Many of the data are not derived from free exchange and free choice; they are politically rigged. Numerous prices for goods and services are arbitrarily set by government or by politically powerful pressure groups: minimum wages, maximum rent, ceilings on earnings, interest, transportation charges, and so on. What and how much one may plant on his own land is more and more determined not by free choice but by political decrees backed by police force. The fruits of one's own labor are increasingly siphoned off for urban renewal, paying farmers not to farm, putting men on the moon, subsidies, below-cost pricing of items such as TVA electricity rates, and countless other pet projects. Unpeaceful interventions in the market!

But the signals given off by the present U.S.A. computer reflect the data we force-feed it—in the same manner as any computer. No more judgment is exercised by one than by the other. Many of the data of the U.S.A. market computer are erroneous; the price signals, as stop and go signs, are and must be to some extent misleading; there is a generous portion of GIGO!

When entrepreneurs act on misleading signals, they drain or glut the market; that is, they create shortages or surpluses—phenomena of the rigged, not the free, market. To illustrate: Suppose you were in charge of the boiler room supplying a 70 degree climate to a factory and that you adjusted the heat supply by a thermometer's signals. Now, imagine that someone changes the calibrations so that an actual 70 degree temperature now registers 80 degrees on the distorted scale. There would soon be a shortage of heat in the factory. Or if the actual 70 degrees were made to register 60 degrees, you would send the factory a surplus of heat. Monkeying with the thermometer—rigging, it is called—creates shortages or surpluses.

Observe what happens to the market when the computer's signals (prices) are rigged. Mink coats, for example, are not now in short supply. They are on display in stores throughout the nation. But let the government decree that the ceiling price on mink coats shall not exceed $25 and immediately there will be a shortage of perhaps 50,000,000 mink coats. Why? Because no one wants to sell them for such a price and because there are that many women who have $25 and desire a mink coat! For evidence, merely recall OPA days.

Next, observe how rigging can and does bring about surpluses: Let the government decree "support prices," that is, guaranteed prices over and beyond what a free market computer would signal, and entrepreneurs will produce more than the market will take. This explains why we now cram into ships, warehouses, granaries, and whatever kind of storage government can lay its hands on, some

1,330,000,000 bushels of wheat, more than 205,000,000 pounds of butter, 289,000 pounds of tung oil, 335,000,000 bales of cotton, 1,700,000 gallons of turpentine, 34,140,400,-000 pounds of grain sorghum, 1,412,193,000 bushels of corn —the list grows wearisome![2]

The Russian Market

Consider, third, something very much different, the Russian market computer as it now exists. It is out of kilter and noninstructive simply because practically all data are rigged, riggers being in complete control over there. Free choice is at a minimum. What can be produced and what consumed is politically dictated by the riggers. Prices, too, are rigged; for in a command economy it is not possible for prices to be set in any other manner. Thus, the Russian market computer is fed "garbage in" on so grand a scale that price signals are quite useless as production guides.

The Russians, so far as we can learn, have admitted the free market computer to operate in one tiny segment of their economy. A small fraction of the tillable land is (in effect) privately owned, and freedom of choice is granted as to what's produced and how it is priced. The results, while fantastic, come as no surprise to anyone with an awareness of how freedom principles work when put in practice: Private plots make up only 3 to 5 per cent of Russia's farm land, yet they yield a product astonishingly

---

[2] See *Agricultural Statistics* (U.S. Government Printing Office, Washington, D. C., 1962), p. 632.

out of proportion to that small fraction. In 1959, some 47 per cent of the USSR's meat came from this fraction of land, 49 per cent of the milk, 82 per cent of the eggs, 65 per cent of the potatoes, and 53 per cent of the vegetables.[3]

Within this limited area of choice for the Russians, economic calculation is made easy. They do not know (nor need they know) a thing about the complex data that is fed into their little, isolated market computer. By merely observing a few of its signals—prices—as do those of us privileged to live in freer societies, they know, to some extent, what and what not to produce; that is, they are automatically informed as to the best allocation of their own scarce resources. Aside from this islet of agricultural freedom, economic calculation in Russia is out of the question.[4] As a consequence, nothing better than political calculation—bungling guesstimates—is possible.

The Russian political riggers, in making their guesstimates, do take peeks at the other market computers in the world, most of these others being more or less instructive, depending on the extent to which they are founded on free exchange.[5] For instance, if to remove our own wheat

[3] *The Wall Street Journal*, May 17, 1961, p. 12. Also see "Private Farming Big Aid to Soviet," *The New York Times*, November 28, 1960.

[4] Professor Ludwig von Mises deserves the greatest praise for logically demonstrating that the socialist community is incapable of economic calculation. See his *Socialism* (New Haven: Yale University Press, 1953), pp. 113-122. Refer also to "Soviet Economists Part Company with Marx" by Dr. Trygve J. B. Hoff. *The Freeman,* September, 1960.

[5] Aleksy Wakar and Janusz Zielinski, leading professors of the Central Planning School of Poland, astonishingly for socialists, say, "The best methods of producing a given output cannot be chosen [by social-

glut, brought on by our own political rigging, we offer our surplus at a price below which the Russian Commissars guess it will cost them to raise wheat by slave labor, the Commissars will effect some sort of a deal with us. By so doing they can then force their own wheat-growing slave labor into other endeavors, perhaps into producing military hardware. But the signals from these other market computers are not received *automatically* into the Russian market computer, for it is jammed; if you like, it is surrounded by an Iron Curtain. The Commissars, alone, can hear the signals; but, not being producers, what can they do with them? Any market computer, to function perfectly, must automatically receive all complex data, and this is impossible unless there be freedom in exchange. This prime requirement is not met in the Russian situation since the free flow of goods and services across the borders is no more than a trickle.

Freedom in Exchange

To repeat, the free market computer renders its services for free, and it frees us from the impossible task of collecting billions of flowing data but—and this is the all-

---

ist methods of calculation] but are taken from outside the [socialist] system . . . i.e., methods of production used in the past, or so-called 'advanced' methods of production, *usually taken from the practice of more advanced countries and used as data for plan-building* by the [socialist] country under consideration." (Italics mine.) See *The Journal of the American Economic Association*, March, 1963.

Anyone's concept of correct economic theory will be improved by grasping the significance of economic calculation. For a clear, simple, and excellent explanation see "Play Store Economics" by Dean Russell. *The Freeman*, January, 1964.

important point—*freedom in exchanges* is an absolute, un-modifiable condition. Freedom in exchanges is the key, the secret; a secret, I must add, which is all too well kept!

The secret reveals itself easily enough if we will conceive of human action for what it really is: human energy in motion—a flowing performance. Potential human energy is enormous, and all creative human energy is incalculably varied; there are as many variations as there are persons; no two of these creative energies are alike. However, potential, creative, human energy, to be useful, must become kinetic, flowing, performing energy. But it cannot flow except as it is freely exchangeable.[6] Imagine anyone trying to exist exclusively by his own energy. Were each of us dependent entirely on this type of creative energy, all of us would perish.

To repeat, the reason that the Russian market computer does not and cannot receive accurate data is because the Soviets do not allow freedom in exchange, that is, they do not let world prices freely interact on and influence Russian prices. Their authoritarianism cuts off the current, so to speak. Only a free market price carries an accurate

---

[6] Free exchange can never be wholly squelched, regardless of how powerful the dictatorship. People, to live, will smuggle and form black markets. For instance, it is generally supposed that the useful goods and services in Russia, such as they are, originate with socialism—the Kremlin's rigging. Nothing of the sort! The Russian people are bursting with creative energy. What actually is witnessed in the production of useful goods and services is but the result of pent-up creative energy forcing its way through the political rigging. The Kremlin, being composed of political riggers and not economists, erroneously concludes that the escaping, free energy is its accomplishment! Indeed, if it were not for the fact that most Russians, in most of their dealings, "cheat" against the theoretical communist system, they would all starve to death.

and instructive message for future production and exchange.

The point is clear enough if we keep in mind that only free exchange data accurately reflect value, *the value of any good or service being what others will give for it in willing exchange*. Data founded on unwilling or unfree (rigged) exchange carry no value messages; it is "garbage in" and, thus, valueless.

A Russian or Polish Commissar, for instance, can be informed of U.S.A. prices—signals from the U.S.A. market computer—in a fraction of a second. Yet, if these prices of ours are founded on rigged data and fed into our own market computer—such as our wheat prices—the rapid communication is nothing but the speedy communication of GIGO. Only if U.S.A. prices are based on free exchange do they have useful instruction to us, to the Russians, or to any other people. To confirm this important point, reflect on how completely we dismiss Russian prices. They have no instruction for us whatsoever, indeed, not even for the Russians themselves—except in the case of their little, free market plots. The distinction between Russian and U.S.A. price signals is that theirs are founded entirely on GIGO, ours only partially so. Were giant Russia a free port, like little Hong Kong, all the world would look to Russian prices for instruction. When we wish to know the real value of gold, for instance, we ask its price where it is freely traded, where there is freedom in exchange. Were all the world's gold freely exchangeable, the market computer would give us a precise, accurate, and instructive answer as to its value. (This is not to say that governmental intervention has no effect on prices; it most certainly has. But the effect is in the form of misleading, not instructive, prices and value.)

Before presenting some work-a-day examples of the market-as-computer concept, it is relevant to ask how many market computers presently exist. Were there no rigging at all in our or any other country—that is, were freedom in exchange universal—there would be but a single, universal market computer. All the data flowing into it would be accurate as would the signals in the form of prices. However, economic understanding is and always has been faulty; thus, no such market computer has ever existed nor is it likely to. The ideal has never been permitted; so, in its stead, we have literally thousands of market computers, the GIGO factor ranging from fractional to complete. If economic understanding advances, the number of market computers will lessen and their performance will improve. We can hope for nothing more than moving toward the ideal.

The Provisioning of Paris

Now for an example by Frederic Bastiat, a remarkably astute economic observer. Certainly, the French market computer of 1846 was considerably rigged; yet, relative to others at that time and since, it was in good working order. Wrote Bastiat:

> On entering Paris, which I had come to visit, I said to myself—Here are a million of human beings who would all die in a short time if provisions of every kind ceased to flow towards this great metropolis. Imagination is baffled when it

tries to appreciate the vast multiplicity of commodities which must enter tomorrow through the barriers in order to preserve the inhabitants from falling prey to the convulsions of famine, rebellion, and pillage. And yet all sleep at this moment, and their peaceful slumbers are not disturbed for a single instant by the prospect of such a frightful catastrophe. On the other hand, eighty provinces have been labouring to-day, without concert, without any mutual understanding, for the provisioning of Paris. How does each succeeding day bring what is wanted, nothing more, nothing less, to so gigantic a market? What, then, is the ingenious and secret power which governs the astonishing regularity of movements so complicated, a regularity in which everybody has implicit faith, although happiness and life itself are at stake? That power is an absolute principle, the principle of *freedom in transactions.* . . . In what situation, I would ask, would the inhabitants of Paris be if a minister should take it into his head to substitute for this power the combinations of his own genius, however superior we might suppose them to be—if he thought to subject to his supreme direction this prodigious mechanism [market computer], to hold the springs of it in his hands, to decide by whom, or in what manner, or on what conditions, everything needed should be produced, transported, exchanged, and consumed? Truly, there may be much suffering within the walls of Paris—poverty, despair, perhaps starvation, causing more tears to flow than ardent charity is able to dry up; but I affirm that it is probable, nay, that it is certain, that the arbitrary intervention of government [rigging] would multiply infinitely those sufferings, and spread over all our fellow-citizens those evils which at present affect only a small number of them.[7]

Few of us, when viewing Paris or New York City or our home town, ever discern the miracle wrought by freedom in exchange as clearly as did Bastiat. Nor do we readily

---

[7] This extract is from *Social Fallacies,* Register Publishing Company edition, 1944.

see that such a fantastic performance as the automatic provisioning of Paris could never be turned over to a government official and his minions without disaster. These people from the eighty French provinces were unaware of what the other millions of producers and distributors were doing; they had no firsthand knowledge of the shifting in tastes and fancies of Parisian consumers. Of the countless data, these anonymous producers knew nothing. All they did was to let their own self-interest respond to the market computer's relatively few signals: prices. Their instructions were received from prices. To the extent that the prices were reflections of free exchange data, to that extent were the instructions faithful guides. To the extent that the data were rigged, to that extent were the instructions misleading. That the data were more right than wrong is self-evident: the million people in Paris were provisioned with no more thought on the part of each than you or I give to the supplying of a restaurant in Hong Kong where we plan to dine next month.

Nor need we confine our reflections to such miracles as the provisioning of cities. What about producing a jet plane or an automobile or a ball-point pen? No single person on earth knows how to make any one of these or tens of thousands of other fabricated items by which we live. The participants in the making of a cup of coffee— growers, makers of bags, and so on by the thousands—are not, by and large, even aware of each other's existence. They do not work as a coffee committee or in conscious concert. With no attention to or thought of each other, these countless producers and distributors merely watch prices: stop and go signals from the market computers. Presto! We who want coffee have it on our tables with no more part in it than the brewing, and voluntarily parting with a fraction of our income: willing or free exchange.

No Rigging in Free Market

The market is a computer; the rigged market is GIGO to the extent that it is rigged and, thus, to that extent, imperfect. The free market is the perfect computer. This is not the claim of a partisan but hard fact. It merely means that values—as determined by willing exchange—are computed freely, that is, without intervention, distortion, rigging. To assert that the free market is the perfect computer is as axiomatic as asserting that a flow is perfectly free if wholly unobstructed.

Computers, with the speed of light, give impersonal answers or signals from the data fed to them. Men, like mice gnawing among the labyrinth of wires in a telephone exchange, can and do rig and, thus, distort, disfigure, and destroy many of the data. The motives for so doing include protection against competition, a belief that value is determined by the amount of effort exerted, a falsely presumed ability to run the lives of others, a conviction that the communistic maxim "from each according to ability, to each according to need" can be administered by force without injustice, the insistence on feathering one's own nest at the expense of others, and countless additional motivations. But, regardless of the reasons, the rigger imposes his errant ways on all the rest of us; he plays authoritarian!

The free market computer is the Golden Rule in economic practice. Value has nothing whatsoever to do with effort exerted; value is what others will willingly exchange for one's goods or services. The market respects the wishes and performances of everyone impersonally. There are no favorites. It is the only means there is for the automatic and speedy allocation of scarce resources; that is, it is the method for bringing a scarce and high-priced good or service within the reach of those whose incomes are lowest. It is the miracle worker, demonstrated daily, over and over again, before our eyes.

A free market, of course, is out of the question except among a people who prize liberty and know the imperatives of liberty. Liberty, I must repeat, is not a one-man term but, like the free market, finds its complete realization in universal practice: every man on earth is born with as much right to his life, his livelihood, his liberty as I. No one can rationally prize liberty for himself without wishing liberty for others.

To realize liberty, to tear ourselves loose from political rigging, to unshackle creative energy, to achieve freedom in transactions, does not, as many contend, require that the individual wait until all others take these steps in unison with him. Implicit in such a council of delay is the taking of no steps by anyone, and this is fatal to liberty. An individual can stand for liberty all by himself; a nation can practice liberty to its own glory and strength though all other states be slave. The blessings of liberty are conferred on all who live by her credo; and basic to liberty is the unrigged market computer.

CHAPTER 14

MAIL BY MIRACLE

MY FELLOW PANELIST, a college dean who espoused government security programs of all sorts, had never before encountered anyone who insisted that government should be limited, without exception, to keeping the peace. Finally, in exasperation, he delivered this intended *coup de grace*: "Well, if my panelist friend thinks that government should be so severely limited, I would like to have him tell this audience how private enterprise could deliver the mail."

He was voicing a common sentiment: Private enterprise deliver the mail? Preposterous! Also, this dean of Labor and Industry was revealing a shocking and common lack of understanding as to how the market works. It is this widespread failure to grasp the miracle of the market which accounts, in no small measure, for the mass turn toward socialism. If there is no faith in getting jobs done by men acting freely, privately, cooperatively, competitively, willingly, voluntarily, peacefully, to that extent will people believe in political authority to guide human action. It's either peace or force; there is no in-between!

Let your imagination take you back just one century, to the year 1864. Suppose, at that time, you had been asked to select the easiest of the following assignments:

1. Deliver the mail;
2. Deliver the human voice a thousand miles;
3. Deliver a dozen individuals from San Francisco to Miami in one day;
4. Deliver an event visually a mile from where it takes place, at the time of its occurrence.

Which of the four would have seemed easiest to accomplish in 1864? Number 1, for certain! Numbers 2, 3, and 4 would then have appeared utterly impossible, too fantastic to be taken seriously. The easiest one of the four—delivery of the mail—has been left in the hands of government. Numbers 2, 3, and 4 have been dealt with so competently and expansively in the free market that we have taken them for granted; we never give them a second thought. So, let us ask, how well has government handled the mail?

For all practical purposes, the government uses the same methods of gathering, sorting, and delivering the mail that it did 100 years ago.

The mail is slower today than it was before World War II.

A letter often takes 48 hours to travel 100 miles.

The Post Office is floundering in a sea of mail that gets deeper every year.

Rates on first-class mail have been hiked 150 per cent since 1932, yet the deficit for the mail operation is now running close to $1,000,000,000 a year, about $3,000,000 for each working day, or ten times what it was in 1932.

Almost all proposals for solving this generally acknowledged bureaucratic failure are predicated on government's remaining in the mail business, as though this were as proper a function of government as is keeping the peace. Proposed solutions range all the way from getting a more competent Postmaster General to appropriating millions of dollars for research, all aimed at the hopeless objective of making a government enterprise efficient.

The Constitution Says So

There are numerous reasons why most people assume that government ought to be responsible for mail delivery. One is this: At our nation's outset, the most respected of American political instruments, *The Constitution of the U.S.A.*, proclaimed, "The Congress shall have power . . . to establish post offices. . . . " The Congress exercised this power. There are now nearly 40,000 post offices.

But Congress went further than the permissibility granted by the Constitution. Congress outlawed competition; it declared mail delivery a government monopoly. No one, today, may carry first-class mail for pay except on a subcontract arrangement with Uncle Sam. The mail business is the government's—period!

When any activity has been monopolized by government for years, persons with entrepreneurial aptitudes rarely think of it as an opportunity for private enterprise. The enterpriser seldom spends any time trying to think how to do something that he will never have a chance to try. An activity monopolized by government soon becomes both "untouchable" and "unthinkable." Thus, everyone—almost —assumes the mail business to be a proper function of government.

Almost! Now and then, however, there are individuals who question the generally accepted premise. Their reasoning goes something like this: More pounds of fresh milk are delivered every day than pounds of mail. Fresh milk is more perishable than a love letter or a catalogue or an appeal for funds or a picture magazine or an entertainment journal. Fresh milk delivery is more efficient, more prompt, lower priced than mail delivery. Why shouldn't men in the market place—acting privately, competitively, voluntarily, cooperatively, peacefully—deliver mail? They deliver freight, which is heavier.

Not only the "man in the street," but a high proportion of enterprisers themselves believe that government should deliver mail. Unwittingly, they have lost faith in themselves as free men to deliver mail. Why?

Free Enterprise Does the Job

First, ask this question: How far could the human voice be delivered 100 years ago? The answer is, the distance two champion hog callers could effectively communicate—about 44 yards. But, left free to try, enterprisers have discovered how to deliver the human voice around this earth, for instance, which is 1,000,000 times as far, and in one-seventh of a second. That's roughly the same time it takes the voice of one hog caller to reach the ear of the other. Quite an accomplishment in delivery, isn't it?

When we have left enterprisers free to try, they have discovered how to deliver a Rose Bowl game, a Shakespearean play, or whatever into everyone's living room in motion and in color at the time it is going on.

When we have left these enterprisers free to try, they have discovered how to deliver 115 individuals from Seattle to Baltimore in less than four hours.

When free to try, they have discovered how to deliver gas from Texas to homes in New York at low cost.

When free to try, they have discovered how to deliver every four pounds of oil from the Persian Gulf to our Eastern Seaboard for less money than government charges to deliver a one-ounce letter from Irvington-on-Hudson to adjacent Tarrytown.

And these are the people—the ones who have had a hand in these miracles—who have lost faith in themselves as free men to deliver letters.

While the last comparison is somewhat loaded, this example of free market oil delivery, on a weight-distance-time basis, wins against the example of mail delivery by more than 10,000 to 1!

Let's try another comparison. The fastest mail service is an airmail letter. With the best of luck a letter posted in Irvington-on-Hudson at 5 p.m. could be in the hands of an addressee in Los Angeles 40 hours later, and for 8 cents. Now, consider the incomparably more complex problem of a personal conversation with the same Angelino. He can be reached and a three-minute talk-fest completed in three and one-fourth minutes, and for $2.25 (plus tax). True, this is 30 times more costly but 750 times faster!

Interestingly enough, the A.T. & T., by far the largest of the human voice communicators, has, during the period when the Post Office was losing $10,000,000,000, showed a profit of $22,000,000,000.

In the light of overwhelming evidence on every hand, why does anyone cling to the notion that a letter can be delivered only by a governmental agency? Instead, we should marvel that people in government are able to deliver the mail at all; not because they are less talented than the A.T. & T. folks, but simply because of the manner in which they are organized to do the job.

Suppose you were asked to head a business—one of the largest in the world—one in which you were wholly inexperienced and to which you had given no thought, as is the case with the mill run of Postmasters General. Next, assume that a substantial part of your key personnel had to be selected on the basis of political preferment. And, finally, imagine that the income of the business depended not on willing exchanges in a free market but on appropriations made to your business by two directorates, of 100 and 435 members respectively (the Senate and House), all having more in mind their own political fortunes than the business for which you have been given responsibility. With responsibility and authority so unrelated, and with the other obstacles mentioned, what kind of a perfotmance do you think *you* could turn in?

Imagine this: A century ago the Post Office—headed, manned, and organized as above—was given a monopoly of all transportation and all communications. What, today, would be the shape of trains, trucks, planes, telephones, wireless, radar had these activities been monopolized as has the mail? Is there any reason to believe that there would have been progress in these technologies? Wouldn't these, like the Post Office, be about as they were 100 years ago?

The Market Not Appreciated

The fact that the Constitution empowered Congress to put government in the postal business does not make it right. The same Constitution condoned slavery.

Nor is government postal service justified by the dangerous and popular notion that government should do for the people that which they cannot or will not do for themselves. If this were a sound rule, then anything the government ever attempted would become a proper government function simply because most people tend to give up— realizing the futility of trying to compete with the tax collector.

Nor can government postal service be justified on the Rural Free Delivery argument. If a person elects to live atop Pike's Peak, let him get his mail as he does his cornflakes or milk or whatever. Why should the rest of us subsidize his desire to have his isolation, and his mail, too?

That mail delivery should be left to the free, competitive market is so buttressed with overwhelming evidence that it is difficult to understand why we persist in our mistake. I have already given some minor reasons; the major reason is failure to understand the miracle of the market.

Omit those inexperienced in business and ask only of outstanding enterprisers, "Should mail delivery be left to the market?" Except in rare instances, their answers will be an emphatic "No!" Their thought processes go something like this: "H'm! Let me see. How would I go about delivering mail to nearly two hundred million people? By George, I don't know. If I, a successful enterpriser, don't know, who does? Of course mail delivery should not be left to the market. It's a government job."

No One Needs to Know

The fact is that our enterprising friend could spend the rest of his life reflecting on how he would deliver mail to all the people in the U.S.A. and never would he think how to do it. *What he doesn't understand is that neither he nor any other person can ever know—or needs to know—how to do the job.* Do just two things and witness a miracle:

1. Let the Congress repeal the monopoly now granted to the government, thus permitting anyone to deliver mail for pay who wishes to do so, as unrestricted as grocery delivery; and

2. Let the Congress appropriate no more money to the Treasury for Post Office Department use, and insist that the accounting be on a basis comparable to private enterprise accounting, to include rentals, taxes, and so on, thus requiring the Post Office Department to charge rates that will incur no deficits.

Within a year or two or three government would be out of the mail business, completely out; private enterprise would take over the whole thing, lock, stock, and barrel. Furthermore, mail delivery would become as efficient as is the communication of sound or the delivery of groceries, taken for granted as is the supply of automobiles, without extra burden to taxpayers, and with profit to enterprisers in proportion to their capacity to cut costs and improve service.

Many will ask, how can this possibly happen when no person now knows how to deliver mail? Very well, how do we manufacture 1,600,000,000 wooden lead pencils annually without anyone knowing how to make a pencil? There, in the pencil story, is the answer: tiny, varied, multitudinous know-hows miraculously, spontaneously, automatically configurating—*so long as they are free to do so*—arising from where and in whom no one can remotely guess. There are thousands upon thousands of testimonies to this free market phenomenon all about us, but the miracle is so unobtrusive that, like the air we breathe, we seldom take any note of it. This wonderful mystery, which so few persons grasp, is rooted in nothing more complicated than a faith in free men. Indeed, the reason that a bureaucracy cannot efficiently deliver mail is that the individual know-hows are not free to flow; the governmental system presupposes something that does not exist: a person who knows how to deliver mail.

Some may claim that I am out to abolish the governmental postal service. But I do not consider that a first order of business. I use the postal service to illustrate that any and all men should be permitted to do anything they please, so long as it is peaceful—even deliver mail for pay; that government has no competency beyond keeping the peace. The postal service merely turns out to be the easiest way to make the point—everything about it is so obvious.

CHAPTER 15

WHOSE ACADEMIC FREEDOM?

MANY thoughtful persons, when supplied with the evidence, will agree that a creative activity should be left to free men, with government relegated to keeping the peace; that is, they will agree when the issue is as clear cut as in the case of the postal service. And many also will concede that this same division of functions should apply to countless creative activities: leave productive and creative affairs to free men; leave the inhibiting and penalizing of destructive actions to government.

Of all activities, none is more obviously in the creative category than is education. Based on the above division-of-functions concept, education would be left exclusively to the free market. Yet, there is a firmly rooted popular conviction or belief in government education. Here, in education, we have the contradiction of means and ends in its most pronounced and perhaps its most dangerous form; certainly, in the form most difficult to clarify.

However, the person who argues that anyone should be able to do anything he pleases so long as it is peaceful and that the role of government is only to keep the peace, had better make his case in this difficult area, or retire from the field. And I know of no better place to begin than with the argument which rages around the subject of academic freedom. Whenever an issue is split down the middle and intelligent men of good will are arrayed on either side of the controversy, one conclusion can be reasonably drawn: some basic principle in the argument has been neglected.

Academic freedom has been debated as if it were primarily an ideological or a philosophical problem, whereas, in my view, it is an organizational problem. Whether a teacher be a communist, a socialist, a Fabian, a New Dealer, or their direct opposite, is a matter of secondary concern, unrelated to the real issue of academic freedom. If we were to shift the subject from academic freedom to freedom in the market place and then argue that it mattered whether or not one were a carpenter, a plumber, a farmer, or whatever, we would be on comparably untenable ground.

The Parent-Child Relationship

The confusions about academic freedom may be cleared if we first examine teaching in its simplest form and move from there to more complex forms.

The simplest teaching relationship would exist between parent and child. The parent is responsible for the child, and consequently has authority over the child. The basic principle in all successful organization is that responsibility and authority be commensurate. Any deviation leads to trouble, whether in the simplest relationship between parent and child or in such complex relationships as are found in large corporate organizations. The successful parent-child relationship will find the parent relinquishing authority as the child grows in stature and assumes the responsibilities for his own life. When responsibilities are fully assumed, no parental authority whatsoever should remain. The solution of the academic freedom problem rests squarely on the responsibility-authority principle.

The mother teaching her child, assuming no interference, has perfect academic freedom. She will teach the child precisely what she wants it to learn. Whether the mother is a communist, an anarchist, or of the libertarian persuasion has no bearing on the question of academic freedom.

Now let us take the first step toward complexity: the mother employing an aide, shall we say, a tutor. The responsibility for the education of the child still rests with the mother. And if trouble is not to ensue, the authority also must remain with her. The tutor may or may not share the mother's views about life, education, and social affairs. But regardless of their agreements or differences, the mother should still be in the driver's seat. If she can delegate a portion of her responsibility-authority powers to the tutor, she also should be free to revoke such powers. The power to hire, logically, carries with it the power to fire. If one could only delegate and not revoke, could only hire and not fire, he would be in the absurd situation of having to live all of his lifetime with an ever-growing accumulation of mistakes. If this were the case, who would dare risk employing anyone?

In this mother-tutor-child arrangement, let us assume that the mother is a devotee of socialism and that the tutor turns out, much to the mother's surprise and disgust, to be of the freedom faith—one who believes in no coercion at all to direct the creative activities of citizens within a society. What then? Is the socialist mother obligated to retain the libertarian tutor on the grounds of academic freedom? Whose academic freedom? The mother's or the tutor's? Is the mother, who once had academic freedom in relation to her child, now to be deprived of it because she hired the tutor? Is the tutor's freedom to teach what he pleases to supersede the mother's freedom to have her child taught what she wishes? This anomalous arrangement would have the mother responsible for the education of the child and for paying the tutor, and leave the tutor with authority as to what the child should be taught—the responsibility-authority principle totally violated. Nothing but friction would result, certainly no educational progress.

Tenure vs. Academic Freedom

Libertarian views generally are founded on the belief that each person has an inalienable right to his own life; that he has the responsibility to protect and to sustain his life; and with this goes the corresponding authority to make free choices—no exception! Our tutor, holding such libertarian views, must concede that the socialist mother's academic freedom supersedes his own as it relates to what should be taught the child. That is her business and not his. For him to argue that he can teach her child what he pleases, that she does not have the authority and the right to discharge him lest his academic freedom be violated, is to place the argument on the wrong ground. *Such a claim would be for tenure, not for academic freedom!*

The tutor's academic freedom is in no way violated if the socialist mother chooses to discharge him. He is free to teach his libertarian views to his own children or to the children of parents who may subscribe to the service he is prepared to render. Academic freedom would be violated if one were coerced into teaching what he believed to be wrong—if the libertarian tutor were compelled to teach socialism, or if the socialist mother were compelled to have her child taught libertarian ideas.

The Private School

Numbers can be added to the parent-tutor relationship without altering the responsibility-authority lines. A good example is a school I knew, the Ferris Institute of 1917, long before it became a government school. Mr. Ferris owned the school. There was no Board of Trustees. It was a venture as private as his own home. He employed teachers in accord with his judgment of their competence. He admitted students in accord with his judgment of their worthiness. If he thought he had erred in the selection of a teacher, the teacher was discharged. And many students were sent home because they would not meet the standard of hard work he required.

Mr. Ferris had the sole responsibility for the success of Ferris Institute; and, correctly, he assumed the authority for its conduct. Academic freedom was in no way offended. Teachers who shared his educational principles were free to submit their credentials and, if employed, to put these principles into practice. Parents who liked the hard-work standards of Ferris Institute were free to seek admission for their children.

Most private educational organizations are more complex than was the Ferris Institute of that time. Some are corporations organized for profit, in which case the ultimate responsibility and authority rest with the stockholders in proportion to their ownership. As a rule, the responsibility and authority are delegated to a Board of Trustees; and the Board, in turn, delegates the responsibility and authority to a chief executive officer, usually a president. The president organizes the institution and delegates the responsibility and authority vested in him to numerous subadministrators and teachers. The stockholders, having the final responsibility for the institution, quite properly have the authority to change Board membership if they find themselves in disagreement with Board policy. The Trustees, in turn, having been given the responsibility by the stockholders, have the authority to discharge the chief executive officer if they believe he is not properly executing its policy. The chief executive officer, vested with responsibility by the Board, has the authority to change his aides if he believes they are not carrying out his ideas. Discretion in exercising authority, regardless of where vested, is assumed.

Complexity in no way alters the responsibility-authority principle, but only increases the difficulty of tracing the responsibility and authority lines.

All organization—educational or otherwise—is an attempt at cooperation. Cooperation is not possible unless responsibility and authority go hand-in-hand. Example: You want a new home, but rather than build your own you select a contractor to whom you delegate the responsibility to build it in conformity with specified plans. Now, suppose that you delegate no authority to the contractor and that other members of your family, and any of the carpenters, can alter the plans at will. The house, if one ever materializes, will be a mess.

Suppose, on the other hand, that you have given the contractor an authority commensurate with his responsibility, and he then tells the carpenters that the construction is to be precisely according to your plans. But the carpenters protest: "This is doing violence to our freedom. You are not letting us practice our views on carpentry." The absurdity of this is apparent. Yet, it is the same as the teacher's protest, "You are doing violence to my academic freedom," when he is asked to respect the authority of the one who has the responsibility for the teaching organization. Actually, he is insisting that he be permitted to do as he pleases in matters for which someone else has the responsibility. He claims freedom to do as he pleases while he denies a like freedom to the responsible person who pays him.

Often, it is not academic freedom that is at issue; it is simply a claim for tenure. American parents, not wanting communism and socialism taught to their children, seek the discharge of teachers of such faiths. But the teachers cry "academic freedom" and the parents, Board members, and school officials are loath to violate this sacrosanct part of their own philosophy. So, the academic freedom argument is a good tenure argument. It is precisely the same as the "right to a job" argument advanced so persuasively by professionals of the labor movement. It "works," and therefore is used.

This argument succeeds because the responsibility-authority principle has been neglected. The neglect comes, in the case of public or, more accurately, government education, because it is most difficult to know who is responsible or what performance is expected. Where does responsibility ultimately rest? With the taxpayers in proportion to their assessments for schools? Generally, this would be denied. With the parents who have children in government schools? These, seemingly, have no more responsibility than those with children in private schools, or than those who have no children at all.

With the voters? Probably this is as close as one can come to identifying ultimate responsibility in the case of government education. If the responsibility rests here, then that is where the final authority rests. It rests here in theory and to some extent in practice. Voters—whether or not they are interested in education and whether or not they have children—elect Boards of Education. These, in turn, select superintendents, who then employ deputies and teachers. Without too much difficulty, one can trace the chain of responsibility in government education from the voters who ultimately hold it and who delegate it by plebiscite to Boards of Education, to superintendents, to teachers. But the teachers, in theory, have no authority to teach what they please. They are, in theory, subject to the authority of the superintendents, the superintendents subject to the Boards, and the Board members to the voters. Simple enough thus far![1]

The question is: What do the voters want taught? What viewpoint has this heterogeneous mass the authority to impose? Every conceivable point of view and educational technique known to man may be found among these millions of voters. They range from one ideological extreme to the other. Among them are communists, socialists of every gradation, anarchists, libertarian idealists, Jews, Catholics, Protestants, and what have you!

What do these people want? They want all things. And the best one can expect from such a plebiscite is the common denominator opinion of the millions, an opinion subject to all sorts of emotional influences, expressed in a voice that is rarely clear.

Lines of Responsibility Tangled

My purpose in this chapter is not so much to show the flaws in government education as to demonstrate how confusion about academic freedom arises when the source of responsibility is unable to speak clearly or exercise the authority it possesses "on paper," that is, in theory.

There need be no such confusion in the case of free market education. Pronounced variation would result were educational endeavors preponderantly private. Each enterprise would present its own brand of education, and customers would take their choice.

---

[1] It is not quite as simple as this suggests. Federal and state and city Departments of Education are assuming increasing powers and tend further to confuse the responsibility-authority lines.

Government endeavor, on the other hand, results in vague generalizations. All the wants and aspirations, the interests and conflicts, are combined into an educational *potpourri,* the ingredients of the compromise being proportional to the popularity of various ideas at the moment.

Adding to the confusion is the fact that all parties in the chain of government responsibility-authority—Boards of Education, superintendents, deputies, and teachers—are themselves voters making decisions not only as a part of the plebiscite but acting on their own authority, not necessarily the authority issuing from the plebiscite.

The government educational effort is a political apparatus and behaves accordingly. The indifference of voters invites special interests to assume command.[2] For instance, if teachers adequately organize, they can easily control the government school system and supplant the voters as the responsibility-authority fountainhead. The deputies, the superintendents, the Boards of Education, and the voters become the teachers' aides, so to speak, helping primarily as taxpayers.

When affairs take such a turn—a common occurrence—it is easy to see how teachers resent any voter interference with the freedom to teach whatever they please. The teachers have appropriated the responsibility for the government schools. And with the responsibility goes the authority to manage the schools, even the authority to make the voters—displaced bosses—pay the bills. In this topsy-turvy

---

[2] Voter indifference today in America is no sociological accident. It is an inevitable consequence of overextended government.

arrangement, it is natural that teachers should feel free to teach what they please. Interference, from whatever source, is indeed a violation of their politically purchased "academic freedom."

As long as education is politically organized, the squabble over academic freedom will continue. The voters, by reason of their natural indifference and diverse opinions, are unlikely to regain the responsibility and authority which the theory of government education presumes to be theirs. If they would end the squabble, they will have to get education out of the political arena.

This confusion about academic freedom, which originates in government education, carries over into private schools in many instances.

Academic freedom is no more sacred than is freedom of speech, freedom of the press, religious freedom, freedom to produce what one pleases, and freedom to trade with whomever one pleases. There is no freedom peculiar to the classroom, diplomas, degrees, or mortarboards. Let anyone teach what he pleases, but let him do it on his own responsibility. Let him not cry "academic freedom" as he robs someone else of freedom.

When government is in the educational driver's seat, academic freedom will always be argued as if it were a political and ideological problem, which really it is not. When the market is free for the production and exchange of all goods and *all* services the issue of freedom—academic, economic, or whatever—is never in question.

CHAPTER 16

EDUCATION FOR
THE SAKE OF OTHERS

THIS chapter is intended as a critique of government education.

The inevitable consequence of governmental intervention in the market—in the areas of food, mink coats, or whatever—is imbalance. That is, when government deviates from its proper role of keeping the peace and invoking a common justice, shortages and surpluses result. As explained in Chapter 13, we are now experiencing a wheat glut by reason of prices rigged by government, known as "support prices." France has a housing shortage because of prices rigged by the French government, known as "ceiling prices."[1] Surpluses and shortages are phenomena of the rigged market, never of the free market. The free market always moves toward equilibrium where supply and demand equate; like water, when free to flow, it moves toward a common level. Balance is the free market's built-in tendency.

---

[1] See the pamphlet, *No Vacancies,* for an account of rent control in France. Single copy on request. Write the Foundation for Economic Education, Inc., Irvington-on-Hudson, New York.

There is governmental intervention in the educational market. We should, therefore, be able to detect surpluses and shortages, that is, imbalance in types of knowledge. There can never be a surplus of knowledge, but there can be—and is—a superfluity of technical know-how relative to general wisdom or understanding. My thesis is that government's intervention in education is, to a marked extent, the cause of a dangerous and grotesque imbalance between these two distinct types of knowledge. In any event, this is the issue here explored.

While few will share my reasons for this imbalance, the fact of imbalance is well known; some writers have stated it impressively:

We have many men of science; too few men of God.
We have grasped the mystery of the atom and rejected the Sermon on the Mount.
The world has achieved brilliance without wisdom, power without conscience.
Ours is a world of nuclear giants and ethical infants.
We know more about war than we know about peace, more about killing than we know about living.[2]

The distortions of civilization now seem to foreshadow the possibility of extinction of our kind.[3]

Man's problems have arisen because his material progress has outstripped his spiritual advancement.[4]

Man must be made to understand that the mechanical transformations he has introduced . . . will mean either progress

---

[2] General of the Army, Omar Bradley. Address, Armistice Day, 1949.
[3] Professor Harlow Shapley, *The View from a Distant Star* (New York: Basic Books, Inc., 1963), p. 92.
[4] Mattie Storms Miller, *Infinite Wisdom,* p. 134.

or ruin according to whether or not they are accompanied by . . . improvement in his moral attitude.[5]

. . . civilization at the moment being in danger of destruction in consequence of an unprecedented development in man's mechanical skill and ability to exploit the forces of nature, with which his ethical sentiments and social wisdom have entirely failed to keep pace.[6]

Reasons for the Imbalance

All of the above are astute and, I believe, important observations.[7] This imbalance in types of knowledge flowing from our vaunted educational system is at once startling and ominous. For never before in history have a people spent as much time in classrooms as do the present generation of Americans. Never as much money spent for education! Never a greater hue and cry for the expenditure of additional billions to finance more of the same! But, significantly, never so much grumbling about the educational results. Quite obviously, there is a common awareness that something is out of kilter, even though there is very little certainty as to what's at the root of it.

Is it not clear that our educational emphasis is more on accumulating know-how than on gaining wisdom or un-

---

[5] Lecomte du Noüy, *Human Destiny* (New York: Longmans, Green & Co., 1947), p. 139.

[6] C. E. M. Joad, *Return to Philosophy* (London: Faber and Faber), p. 177.

[7] I concede that this alleged imbalance between know-*how* and know-*why* rests solely on value judgments and, thus, this analysis can have meaning only to those who, in a general way, share my values. What follows cannot rise above nonsense to those who attach importance only to more and more technological know-how—scientism—and little, if any, importance to understanding and wisdom.

derstanding? Our know-how in the fields of mathematics, physics, chemistry, and other sciences has made possible the hydrogen bomb, as well as the putting of monkeys and men into orbit, and sending TV sets to the moon. Observe the nature of quiz shows and the kudos we heap on masters of current events and the obeisance we pay to those who can recite the encyclopedia. We know how to make clothes out of sand, airplane wings from sea water, utensils from oil. If we don't make silk purses out of sows' ears, it is only because—well, who wants a silk purse? We have know-how galore, giving us enough power to destroy every living thing. Know-how is power, and we tend to worship power.

Lack of Understanding

But where is the understanding to balance the know-how? A breakthrough in know-how appears to have edged wisdom off the driver's seat. For, are we not, as a nation, on the same reckless course that has brought about the fall of one civilization after another? Self-responsibility— amidst an abundance of know-how and a paucity of wisdom, understanding, conscience, ethics, insight—has given way to government responsibility for our security, welfare, and prosperity, reminiscent of the Roman Empire's later days. Unwisely, we increase the curbs on individual initiative. The theme that we can spend ourselves rich has, among "nuclear giants," switched from heresy to orthodoxy; inflation is dreaded and cursed by the very people who, in an utter lack of understanding, promote it. Feathering the nests of some at the expense of others has, in our know-how society, become the chief political preoccupation. Among the "well educated," the number who think of rights to life, livelihood, liberty as deriving from the state, not the Creator, is growing, and integrity gives way to popular acclaim. The directive of one's behavior is less and less what conscience dictates as right and more and more what the gods of fame and fortune decree. A little knowledge may be dangerous, as the saying goes, but a rapidly expanding know-how, unless balanced by a commensurately expanding wisdom, assuredly spells disaster.

Perhaps we can better assess a present position by taking stock of our beginnings. To illustrate: The Bible, filled with much understanding and wisdom—in a very real sense an educational launching pad for Western civilization—was compiled some eighteen to twenty-eight centuries ago.[8] The writers had little of the know-how we possess. Perhaps they never dreamed of, let alone knew, the multiplication table. Of higher mathematics, they were unaware. Zero wasn't invented until centuries after their time. There wasn't a B.A. or Ph.D. among them; indeed, could any Biblical writer have passed one of our eighth grade examinations? Know-how—as we use the term—was not their primary objective, but understanding principles was. They were men of insight and integrity.

The first stage of wisdom requires that we understand the virtues and how to live them. Integrity, that is, fidelity

---

[8] To appreciate the extent of the U.S.A.'s religious heritage and its impact on our Founding Fathers, see *The Christian History of the Constitution of the United States*, compiled by Verna M. Hall.

to one's highest conscience, is foremost and basic. Next is humility—in the sense of freeing oneself from be-like-me-ness. These prime virtues, if understood and practiced, impart a rare wisdom: a sensitive and acute realization that a human being is a man and not a demigod. Without this wisdom, man tends to behave as demigod. And therein, I believe, lies the key to educational imbalance.

No one has ever seen a demigod, except perhaps in the mirror. Thus, a demigod is an error of the psyche, nothing more. But this error must not be discounted; it is widespread and unbelievably powerful. To assess its pervasiveness, merely note the millions of individuals who actually believe that the rest of us would fare better were we a reflection of themselves. Each of these millions would have us live in the kind of housing he has in mind, work the hours he prescribes, receive the wages he thinks appropriate, exchange with whom he decrees and on terms he proposes, but, more particularly, he wants us to be educated as he thinks proper! Bear in mind, however, that not a single one of these millions is a demigod in the judgment of any other person than himself. Perhaps he may never think of himself in such egotistical terms; he merely performs as if he were a demigod: *He would mold us in his own image!*[9] I repeat, this is an error of the psyche, nothing more.

---

[9] This behavior is, of course, egotism in its most destructive form. Instead of seeking self-fulfillment in the development of the individual's moral nature, sense of justice, creativity, such behavior expresses itself in the imposition of the individual's will on others. Only in self-realization can there be growth among the human species; inflicting self on others—the demigod behavior—can result only in stultification.

Just the Two of Us

My hypothesis: Our educational system, to a marked extent, stems from this error of the psyche. If this be demonstrable, then we can account for some of the faults we are finding with the system, the hassles over integration and segregation, prayers in schools, and so on. We will then perceive why we are putting such an emphasis on the acquisition of know-how to the neglect of understanding or wisdom; we will become aware of the corrective steps that must be taken if know-how is to be balanced with wisdom; and we will have the background for not thrusting ourselves further down a dead-end road.

Let us begin an examination of this hypothesis by reducing the problem to manageable proportions: a consideration of only two individuals, you and me. While it is easily demonstrable that I know very little about me and you about yourself, I know more about myself than anyone else does, and I acknowledge that you know yourself better than I know you.

The most important admission to be made at the outset is that you and I are not alike. Our inheritances differ, as do our environments. My aptitudes, faculties, potentialities, likes and dislikes, yearnings, inhibitions, ambitions, capabilities and inabilities to learn about this or that are not at all like yours. As to our common ground, each of us has a moral obligation not to impair the life, livelihood, liberty of others. Beyond this, we must resort to the broadest and more or less irrelevant generalities: we are Americans, we belong to the human species, and so on. We aren't as "two peas in a pod"; we are at variance in every particularity.[10] We not only differ from each other but we don't remain constant ourselves; each of us is in perpetual flux, changing in every respect daily, aging in some ways, growing in others.

In short, we must keep in mind that you and I are unique specimens of humanity; we are peculiarly distinctive; that is, each of us is *an original,* the first and only creation of its likeness in cosmic experience; that nothing identical to either you or me is possible; that neither of us has ever been, is now, or ever will be, duplicated. You, as much as I, are a physical, mental, moral, perceptive, political, and spiritual entity—a *singular* entity—and any carbon copy is out of the question.

Before moving on to the next phase of this analysis, I must ask that you make an extravagant assumption in this you-and-me situation, namely, that I am as knowledgeable and as wise as the most powerful political leader in the nation.[11] Otherwise, I run the risk of my hypothesis being disregarded by reason of my own acknowledged shortcomings.

You Draw on Me

Let us now examine my possible educational relationships to you. At issue are two opposed roles that I might assume. The first and, to me, the proper role is to let you

---

[10] See *Biochemical Individuality* by Roger Williams (New York: John Wiley & Sons, Inc., 1956), pp. 2-3.

[11] I use "most powerful political leader" because, as will be demonstrated, our educational system is, in most essential respects, geared to a political organism.

draw on such know-how and understanding as I may possess and as *you may determine*. Education is a seeking, probing, taking-from process, and the initiative must rest with
the seeker. As great as is my stake in your better education,
I must concede that your progress depends on your desire
to learn, that this inquisitiveness into the nature of things
is a truly spiritual experience—the spirit of inquiry—that
this is *wholly volitional* and that you are the sole possessor
of your volitional stimuli. These, as related to you or *your*
children, are exclusively yours; they do not, they cannot,
rest with me or any other person. Mine is, at best, only
an exemplar's role: it is to improve myself to the utmost
and thus to persuade solely by precept and example. If
it turns out that I have something in store which in your
view—not mine—may lift you or *your* children up another
notch, then my self-interest is served by obliging you. Arranged in this pattern, the student selects his teachers.[12]

If you—regardless of who you are—will confine your
evaluations to the you-and-me situation, that is, if you will
exclude any thought of anyone but the two of us, you will
readily agree that my role, as above portrayed, is a proper
one; it isn't possible for any rational person to conclude
otherwise! In short, you would not have it any other way.
And, further, I am quite certain that when you are at liberty to glean from me or any others as you may choose,
you will obtain for yourself as balanced an educational
diet as is possible for you. As with food for the flesh, so

---

[12] If the student is a child, the selection is made by the parent; for
the child, until reaching the point of self-responsibility, is but an
extension of the parent's responsibility. I expanded on this idea in
Chapter 15.

with sustenance for the intellect and the spirit: you will
be led naturally to select those bits of know-how and wisdom from first this and then that person—a balancing of
these two types of knowledge which will gratify those needs
peculiar only to you among all mankind. You will gravi-
tate in due course toward that balance of know-how and
wisdom needed for the fulfillment distinctive to your own
person.[13] In other words, *you will learn more of what you
want to learn if you are free to choose what you want to
learn than if you are not free to choose what you want to
learn.* This is self-evident; it needs no proof.

I Force You to Learn

My second possible role is that of demigod—the one
currently in vogue and the role here in question. Not that
I am a demigod—no one is—but let us assume that I pose
and behave as one: I shall compel your classroom attendance; write your curriculum in accord with my notions of
your needs and force it upon you; and, lastly, I shall coercively extort the financial wherewithal from all and
sundry to defray the costs of imposing my own peculiar
brand of knowledge upon you. In short, I shall attempt, as
would a demigod, to cast you in my image! Your education for my sake!

---

[13] That wisdom of the ancients—the Biblical writers—which remains as the core of our idealism to this day was, so it appears, come
upon in this free-seeking, self-responsible manner. There was nothing
that qualified as an educational "system." The political establishment
in those centuries was anything but an "aid" to education. The wisdom seems to have come from avid seekers after truth, working on their
own initiative, more self- than other-directed.

Bearing in mind our countless differences, what would you think of my program for making you or *your* children a carbon copy of me? Even conceding that I am as well balanced in know-how and wisdom as our country's most powerful political leader?

In any event, is it not evident that the approach of the demigod—an error of the psyche—is antagonistic to the advancement of wisdom even though some chunks of know-how might be rammed into your reluctant head? Your and my creative peculiarities are so diverse that they cannot mesh; mine cannot be forcibly impressed upon yours without misshaping both yours and mine. It is somewhat analogous to taking a male die and a female die, each made of pliable, delicate material—but not matching—and pressing them together by an external pressure. The uniqueness of each would be destroyed.

Wisdom has its genesis in creative phenomena. Coercion, clearly, is not a creative force; it is, by definition, repressive and destructive. Physical force can no more be used to stimulate the spirit of inquiry or advance wisdom or expand consciousness or increase perception than it can be employed to improve prayer—and for precisely the same reason. Acquiring understanding or wisdom springs from the volitional faculty as does wishing or exercising judgment or contemplating or praying.

Let me repeat, there is not a single demigod on the face of the earth but, unfortunately, millions of human beings behave as if they were God; the you-should-believe-and-behave-as-I-do variety is all about us; indeed, there may be but few persons who have completely shed themselves of this holier-than-thou trait. However, unless these persons go beyond the believing, behaving, talking, writing stage, their image-molding affliction does no more damage than an offensive TV ad: we can tune them out! Their misconception wreaks no more havoc than does other error *as long as their passive image-molding is not activated by coercion.*

The Larger Situation

The you-and-me situation, as above portrayed, will evoke but little disagreement. But get set for a shock! For unless you are one of a very few—a fraction of one per cent—who has thought this problem through to a conclusion, what follows will tend to offend. While I shall do no more than to multiply myself in the role of image-molding-by-force several million times, the mere multiplication—nothing more—will give us a situation that coincides with long established and generally approved American custom. To question "the establishment," in any instance, is to affront the mores, a risky business. However, we should never fear taking a hard look at any rut we may be in.

So here it is: If it is evident that the forcible casting of you or *your* children in my image is wrong, let me suggest that government schooling, practiced here for well over a century, is precisely the same thing, except on the grand scale. Instead of your being cast in the mold of one who has the know-how and wisdom of our most powerful political leader, tens of millions are and have been cast in molds shaped from nondescript plebisicites, each mold being patterned after nothing better than the compromises produced by political committees; all molds shaped by collectives, no member of which has any more sense of responsibility toward any particular individual than does the collective itself. Self-responsibility is not the trait of a committee or collective.

Lest you get the idea that I have made some sort of a shift from the you-and-me arrangement to government schooling, let me hasten to add that the two are identical with respect to the compulsions involved:

a. compulsory attendance;
b. government prescribed curricula; and
c. forcible collection of the wherewithal to defray costs.

I readily concede that a great deal of first-rate education goes on in our government school systems; but I must insist that the first-rate production is in spite of, not because of, the coercive or governmental aspects. Untold millions of teachers and students, in many of their day-to-day relationships, are on a voluntary, not a coercive basis; to a large extent the students are selecting their teachers. But wherever coercion insinuates itself into schooling— that is, the upbringing process—be it government or private, an imbalance of know-how and wisdom will become evident. Wisdom will decrease, not increase, when the reliance is on duplication by force; wisdom cannot be grafted onto a carbon copy.

While it is easy enough to see how wisdom suffers under schooling systems that feature coercion, it is not as easy to understand why know-how thrives so well. Perhaps part of the explanation has to do with that which can be seen and that which cannot be seen. The multiplication table, for example, can be and is "learned by heart" by those who are compelled to attend classes. Insight, however, the mother of wisdom, is of a different order and cannot be so induced. But—here's the rub—neither can invention (from which stems our enormous know-how) be so induced.

Subsidized Inventors

How, then, can coercion stimulate the know-how type of inventiveness? No one can be coerced to invent, for inventiveness belongs to the creative order. Nor is compulsory invention attempted. The mystery is not too difficult to unravel: billions of dollars are *coercively* collected from all of us—limiting our individual pursuits—and used to pay for government's know-how pursuits such as science, war hardware, moon machinery, and so on. No government regime is capable of inducing wisdom and would not know what to do with it in any event. An expansion of know-how and the power it gives is what's politically attractive. Further, *inventors are as creative if paid by coercively collected funds as if paid by voluntarily contributed funds:* He who pays the fiddler calls the tune. Government calls for know-how and gets it. Compulsion—government intervention in the educational market—accounts, in no small measure, for the imbalance of know-how and wisdom.

Some, at this point, will counter with the argument that we have many private institutions and that the students from these are no more distinguished for wisdom than those graduated from government institutions. The point is conceded. But so-called private institutions in a statist society are not, in fact, strictly free-market in character. Not only must they liken themselves markedly to "big brother" and devote much time teaching about the economics and philosophy of statist institutions, but they are licensed and regulated and increasingly financed by their statist "competition." So-called private institutions differ from government institutions in that they are not financed exclusively by tax funds, and the government influence on them is exerted by privately as distinguished from governmentally appointed citizens. In most important respects the "private" and government institutions are strikingly alike today—a drab conformity. In a society where education is preponderantly statist and where so much of the nation's resources are converted to know-how pursuits, the situation could not be otherwise.

The Wrong Turn

Finally, it would seem appropriate to inquire how we in the U.S.A. got off on the wrong foot; how did we, in the first place, ever acquire an educational system that turns out graduates who acknowledge its many faults and who instead of looking for something out of kilter merely insist on remedy by expansion?

History reveals the original "reasoning" to have been somewhat as follows: America is to be a haven for free men. To accomplish this, we must have a people's, not a tyrant's government. However, such a democratic plan will never work unless the people are educated. But free citizens, left to their own resources, will not accomplish their intellectual upbringing. Therefore, "we" must educate "them": compulsory attendance in school, government dictated curricula, forcible collection to defray the costs. In short, *education for the sake of others.*

Of course, the early proponents of government education never put the case in these concise terms. Had they done so, they would have discovered, at the outset, how illogical they were. Imagine: *We will insure freedom to "the people" by denying freedom to them in education, for if their education is entrusted to freedom they will remain uneducated and, thus, will not be able to enjoy the blessings of freedom!* Illogical? How can we ever expect a people brought up on coercion to be free of demigod mentalities? Does a coercive educational system have the intellectual soil and climate where freedom and wisdom may flourish? The answers lie all about us.

Some of our forefathers did behave—indeed, even as you and I—like demigods, but "for the good of all," mind you! And in the name of doing good—occasionally erring as do we all—they hooked up coercion to the spirit of inquiry and got for themselves and their posterity a grotesque imbalance of know-how and wisdom. Assuredly, any light that coercion produces is not in the form of wisdom.

Once on this coercive trek toward "nuclear giants and ethical infants"—toward know-how in everything and understanding in nothing—how do we back out of it? The steps are simple enough to designate, if not to take; but reaching our goal may take a bit of time. How long? Nothing less than the hours or days or years you and I and others need to recover from our demigod pose—nothing less than the time it takes to reject compulsion and to accept liberty in education. How, any rational person must ask, can a people be free or wise unless they are brought up in, steeped in, believe in, and understand that growth in wisdom presupposes freedom of the individual to pursue what is wise? As the present imbalance between know-how and wisdom has its genesis not with government but with individuals who make government what it is, so a balancing of these two types of knowledge rests with individuals— with those who can see as imperative the practice of freedom in education.

• **CHAPTER 17** •

EDUCATION FOR
ONE'S OWN SAKE

THIS CHAPTER is intended to suggest free market education as the appropriate alternative to government education.

In previous chapters I have tried to demonstrate that government is organized police force and that its function is to keep the peace; that education is a peaceful, creative, productive pursuit of the type disastrously affected by government intervention. Now, were government to step aside in education as it has stepped aside in religion—that is, if compulsory attendance, state dictated curricula, and forcible collection of the wherewithal to pay the school bill were omitted—education would be left to the free market.

Were this break with tradition to take place, what would happen?

Strange as it may first appear, *no one can know!* Some will say that this admission is a retreat from my argument that education would be improved if left to the free, competitive market. On the contrary, it is in support of the free market as the sole, effective means of improving education.

If you are compelled to do as someone else dictates, if

unnatural obstacles are placed in your way, if you are relieved of responsibilities, I can at least predict that you
will not function to your fullest in a creative sense. But
no one can even roughly predict what wondrous things
you will create if released from restraints and dictation,
that is, if freed from obstacles. Indeed, you cannot make
such predictions about yourself. What new idea will you
have tomorrow? What invention? What will you do if a
new necessity, an unexpected responsibility, presents itself?
We know that creativity will be increased, nothing more.

Confining the discussion to education, assume that you
are no longer compelled to send Johnnie to school; no
government committee will prescribe what Johnnie must
study; no government tax collector will take a penny of
your or anyone else's income for schooling. This, it must
be emphasized, is the free market assumption.

Is Johnnie in any less need of learning than before? Are
other persons—teachers, for instance—any less wise or less
available for counsel and employment? Is there less money
for educational purposes? If no longer compelled to pay
the money in taxes, would you spend it on parties or
cigarettes or alcohol or vacations rather than voluntarily
spending it for Johnnie's education? If so, you value Johnnie's education less than you value indulging yourself. In
any event you make a choice—a choice that you obviously
think to be the better alternative; scarcely anyone would
claim that he had decided to choose what he values least
when he could choose what he values most.

Shall we say someone else thinks your judgment is bad
if you decide in favor of vacations, for instance, as against

Johnnie's education? Do you wish the person who thinks your choice is wrong forcibly to impose his notion of right on you? If so, just where are you going to draw the line as to what choices others are to make for you? To authorize others to make your choices is to put yourself in the role of an automaton. You can't believe that your choice is best and accept, at the same time, someone else's verdict that it is the worst. This is utter nonsense. To apply police force to you is to contradict your judgments. If applied to others, it can only contradict their judgments. Who is the appropriate ruler of your educational program? You? Or others? Or a political committee which cannot be better than the lowest common denominator of others?[1] The free market way relies not on one judgment for the millions but on millions of individual judgments.

Religious Freedom

Why should not education be just as self-determined as religion? Is education more important than religion? Americans condemn Russians, for instance, more for being ungodly than for knowing how to make little else than vodka and caviar that can compete in international trade. But do we not emulate the communists by favoring the employment of force in education? Applying police force to education is man playing at god, that is, trying to cast others in his own fallible image.

In the United States, we have rejected the use of the police force for the purpose of determining one's religion.

---

[1] Refer to Chapter 8.

Are high moral standards and improving attitudes toward one's life and the life of others—prime objects of religion —of less value than knowing how to read or to write or to add two and two? Indeed, are not both education and religion intimately personal matters, one as much as the other? Is the education of another any more of my or your business than the religion of another?

In many countries—certainly in the U.S.A.—the idea of (1) being compelled by government to attend churches, or (2) having the government dictate clergymen's subject matter, or (3) having the expenses of religious institutions forcibly collected by the tax man, would be an affront to the citizens' intelligence. Why do people believe in applying police force to education and letting religion rest on self-determination? Logically, there appears to be no basis for the distinction. Tradition, custom—living with a mistake so long that reason is rarely brought to bear— may be the explanation.

Being a disbeliever in the management by the police force of any creative activity, I have on countless occasions asked individuals in various occupational levels if they would let their children go uneducated were all governmental compulsions removed. The answers given me have always been in the same vein. If you will try this yourself, you will be impressed with how alike the answers are: "Do you think I am a fool? I would no more let my children go without an education than I would let them go without shoes and stockings. *BUT* some forms of compulsion are necessary, for there are many persons who do not have the same concern for their children as I have."

And there you have it! Police force is never needed to manage my education, only necessary for the other fellow! The other fellow's weakness—the possibility of his having no interest in himself or in his offspring—is far more imaginary than real. It is, for the most part, a fiction of the compulsory, collectivistic myth. Should you doubt this, try to find that rare exception, "the other fellow." If every parent in this country were to consider authoritarianism in education as applying only to himself and could divorce from his thinking the "incompetency of others," there would be no police force applied to American education. Let any reader of this thesis, regardless of wealth status, honestly try this exercise and arrive at any other conclusion!

A Parental Responsibility

A child, from the time of birth until adulthood, is but the extension of the parent's responsibility. The child can no more be "turned out to pasture" for his education than for his morals or his manners or his sustenance. The primary parental responsibility for the child's education cannot properly be shifted to anyone else; responsible parenthood requires that some things remain for one's own attentions, no matter how enticingly and powerfully specialization and division of labor may beckon one. And, the education of one's children is a cardinal case in point.

This does not mean parents should not have help—a lot of specialized assistance—with their educational responsibility. It does mean that the parent cannot be relieved of the educational responsibility without injury to himself—that is, without injury to his own person and thus to the child who is but the extension of his personal responsibility.

According to the premise on which all of my own positions are based, man's highest purpose in life is the unfolding of his own personality, the realization, as nearly as possible, of his creative potential, that is, his emergence, his hatching, his becoming. Such achievement presupposes that the educational process will go on through all of adulthood, as well as during childhood. Indeed, school for the child, if it is to have meaning, is but the preparation for a dynamic, continuing process of education. The test of whether or not any primary and secondary educational system is meeting the requirements of true education is: Does it set the stage for adult learning?

Police Force Interjected

How does the application of police force to education bear on this question? It tends to relieve parents of educational responsibilities, including the study that might have involved themselves. Compulsion—police force as boss— says, in effect, to the parent: "Forget about the education of your child. We, acting as government, will compel the child to go to school regardless of how you think on the matter. Do not fret unduly about what the child will study. We, the agents of compulsion, have that all arranged. And don't worry about the financing of education. We, the personnel of authority, will take the fruits of the labor of parents and childless alike to pay the expenses. You, the parent, are to be relieved of any choice as to these matters; just leave it to the police force."

Second, these police force devices falsely earmark the educational period. They say, ever so compellingly, that the period of education is the periód to which the compulsion applies. The ceremonies of "graduation"—diplomas and licenses—if not derivatives of this system, are consistent with it. Government education is resulting in young folks coming out of school thinking of themselves as educated and concluding that the beginning of earning is the end of learning. If any devotee of government education will concede that learning ought to continue throughout all of life, he should, to be consistent, insist on compulsion for adults as well as for children—for the octogenarian as well as for the teenager. The system that is supposed to give all an equal start in life tends to put an end to learning just at the time when the spirit of inquiry should begin its most meaningful growth.[2]

---

[2] "The normal human brain always contains a greater store of neuroblasts than can possibly develop into neurons during the span of life, and the potentialities of the human cortex are never fully realized. There is a surplus and, depending upon physical factors, education, environment, and conscious effort, more or less of the initial store of neuroblasts will develop into mature, functioning neurons. The development of the more plastic and newer tissue of the brain depends to a large extent upon the conscious efforts made by the individual. There is every reason to assume that development of cortical functions is promoted by mental activity and that continued mental activity is an important factor in the retention of cortical plasticity into late life. Goethe . . . [and others] are among the numerous examples of men whose creative mental activities extended into the years associated with physical decline. . . . There also seem sufficient grounds for the assumption that habitual disuse of these highest centers results in atrophy or at least brings about a certain mental decline." Renee von Eulenburg-Wiener, *Fearfully and Wonderfully Made* (New York: The Macmillan Company, 1939), p. 310.

A Faith in Freedom

It was stated above that no one could know what would happen were there to be no more police-force-as-boss in education. That assertion is correct concerning specifics and details, but there are generalizations which can be confidently predicted. For instance, one knows that creative energies would be released; that latent potential energies would turn to flowing, moving, power-giving, kinetic energies and activities. Creative thought on education would manifest itself in millions of individuals. Such genius as we potentially and compositely possess would assert itself and take the place of deadening restraints. Any person who understands the free market knows, without any qualification whatsoever, that there would be more education and better education. And a person with a faith in free men is confident that the cost per unit of learning accomplished would be far less. For one thing, there wouldn't be any police boss to pay for. Nor would there be the financial irresponsibility that characterizes those who spend other people's money. The free market is truly free.[3]

Not only is this faith in uninhibited, creative human energy rationally justified, but also there is evidence aplenty to confirm it. In other words, this faith is supported both theoretically and pragmatically. Except in the minds of those who are temperamentally slaves—those who seek a shepherd and a sheep dog, those who are ideologically attuned to authoritarianism—there does not exist a single creative activity now being conducted by man in voluntary

---

[3] Refer to Chapter 13.

action that could be improved by subjecting it to the police-force-as-boss. But put any one of these activities, now voluntarily conducted, under government control, leave it there for a short period, and general opinion would soon hold that the activity could not be conducted voluntarily.

A couple of decades from now, after the electric power industry has been nationalized for a few years—a likely event if present trends continue—there will be only a few people in America who will favor a return to private ownership and operation. The vast majority will not understand how that activity could exist without policeforce-as-boss and still serve the people. For confirmation of this point, reflect again on the many people today who believe that the relatively simple matter of mail delivery could not be left to the free market without resulting in chaos.

It is a separation from reality, a blindness to the enormous evidence in support of freedom—like being unaware of our autonomic nervous system and its importance—that accounts for much of our loss of faith in the productivity of an educational system relieved of restraints and compulsions. The restraints, be it remembered, are in the form of taxes—the taking away of the wherewithal to finance one's own educational plan. The compulsions are in the form of forced attendance and dictated curricula.

Several aids to the restoration of a faith in free market education are:

1. Observe activities not yet socialized—that is, not conducted by police-force-as-boss—and how satisfied we are with

free market operation. And also note that people fare better in countries that are more free than in countries that are less free —without exception!

2. What is there which we know how to do, and for which there is an effective demand, which remains undone in America? Not a thing except that which police force restricts. There are many thousands of individuals expert in educational techniques.

Effective demand? Can anyone argue plausibly that there can be education of those who do not want it? The answer is the same as to the question, "What can anyone force another to learn?" You can push a pupil into a classroom, but you can't make him think. Those who want education—and they can never get it if they do not want it—will have education. Authoritarianism is antagonistic to the extremely sensitive spirit of inquiry, the will to learn. Remove all police-force-as-boss, and we remove education's chief obstacle.

3. While one cannot know of the brilliant steps that would be taken by millions of education-conscious parents were they and not the government to have the educational responsibility, one can imagine the great variety of cooperative and private enterprises that would emerge. There would be thousands of private schools, large and small, not necessarily unlike some of the ones we now have. There would be tutoring arrangements of a variety and ingenuity impossible to foresee. No doubt there would be both profit-making and charitably financed institutions of chain store dimensions, dispensing reading, writing, and arithmetic at bargain prices. There would be competition, which is cooperation's most useful tool.[4] There would be alertness of parents as to what the market would have to offer. There would be a keen, active, parental responsibility for their children's and their own growth. Socialism would be explained but seldom advocated in the classroom. The free market, by its nature, would rule out such waste and

---

[4] Without competition among bakers, for instance, I have no basis for deciding on the baker with whom I will exchange, that is, cooperate.

extravagance. Competition for the educational dollar would attend to that.

4. Let your imagination take you back to 1900. Suppose someone had been able to conjure up a picture of a 1964 automobile with all of its wonderful performances. And suppose you had been asked how it could have been made. You could not even have grasped such a miracle, let alone have described how to make it. Yet, it has been produced, and without police-force-as-boss. Indeed, what would the 1964 car be like if the government had compelled attendance at research laboratories, dictated the subjects to be explored and the wonders to be invented, and forcibly collected the funds for the undertaking?[5]

Bear in mind that millions of unobstructed man-hours of ever-improving skills and thought, in a constant and complex free exchange process and with a strict attention to millions of individual judgments, have made the 1964 car so useful to so many people. And so it would be with free market education. We cannot foretell what would happen if free men were responsible for this activity; that is, if as much creative, uninhibited thought—in response to consumer wants—were put into education as has been put into motor cars.

As it is, a vast majority of the people have given little more than cursory thought as to how to educate without employing police-force-as-boss. No wonder! We have the tendency not to think about problems not our own, about activities pre-empted by government. Remove the obstacles of coercion and the potential energy of man will approach realization. Police-force-as-boss as an effective means to the educational end is but a superstition. It has no foundation in fact.

5. The children of the poor? They obtained food and clothing prior to our practice of governmental alms—more than ever available before. But education isn't as important as shoes and stockings? Education is only as important as life itself. Johnnie couldn't get a job as truck driver unless able to

---

[5] I suspect it would be about as remote from consumer requirements as the vehicle now being built to put men on the moon.

read street signs or bills of lading. Furthermore, remove the taxes we are now paying for present governmental interventions—including education—and poor parents will not be as poor. And literally millions of Americans would like nothing better than voluntarily to finance the education of children of those who might be in unfortunate circumstances.

Some, of course, will counter with the notion that receiving such charity is degrading, an unforgivable socialistic cliché.[6] No one argues that voluntary giving is degrading; all consider giving as a brotherly act. Does not giving presuppose a recipient? Can giving be brotherly and receiving degrading? True, perhaps charity isn't as agreeable to a recipient as self-financing, but is it not more agreeable than police grants-in-aid?

If government were out of education as its boss—100 per cent—and if we had only free market education, no child in America would be denied an education any more than any child is presently denied religious instruction or shoes and stockings.

The Tendency Toward Anarchy

While the above case for free market education is good enough for me, I confess to a practical dilemma. Regardless of the attempts throughout history to limit police force to its role of keeping the peace—a societal guard, so to speak—it has always gotten out of hand. Sooner or later, in every instance, the role has been shifted from guard to boss of the citizenry, that is, from people service to people control; protector turned predator, one might say! So sad is the record of limitation that some persons throw up

---

[6] Scholarships—how do they differ?—are sought and granted on an enormous scale by the very persons who repeat this cliché.

their hands in despair, incorrectly concluding that if limitation has never been maintained, it, therefore, is forever impossible. They begin to disbelieve even in government as peace keeper, insisting on no government at all; they become what might be called philosophical anarchists.

The reason for unsuccessful limitation is that too few individuals have ever understood the price that must be paid for limitation. The price is far more than writing a Constitution and a Bill of Rights with their proscriptions against governmental excesses, and designing a government of checks and balances. The price is the resurrection of what has become a bromide into a living, dynamic performance: *eternal vigilance.*

This performance is in the form of an achievement in understanding (1) the nature of government, (2) its uniqueness as police force, and (3) the limited competence of, as well as the absolute necessity for, police force—an understanding to be learned, mastered, and remembered by at least enough persons to form an effective leadership in each new generation. This performance is a personal, day-in and day-out requirement, meaning that it cannot be delegated to others, much less to our forefathers; it can never be relegated to the past tense; it is a *continuing* imperative of each new moment, without end.

The dilemma is this: The understanding of police-force-as-guard will, obviously, never be advanced but only retarded when the police-force-as-boss is put in the educational driver's seat. Thus, unless a breakthrough is achieved by an individual here and there, capable of independent analysis and unafraid of parting company with the mores, the most important aspect of education for responsible citizenship will go unattended.

The myth of government education, in our country today, is an article of general faith. To question the myth is to tamper with the faith, a business that few will read about or listen to or calmly tolerate. In short, for those who would make the case for educational freedom as they would for freedom in religion, let them be warned that this is a first-rate obstacle course. But heart can be taken in the fact that the art of becoming is composed of acts of overcoming. And becoming is life's prime purpose; becoming is, in fact, enlightenment—self-education, its own reward.

CHAPTER 18

IN PURSUIT OF EXCELLENCE

THE IDEAL OF FREEDOM is to let anyone do anything he pleases, as long as his behavior is peaceful, with government empowered to keep the peace—and nothing more. An ideal objective, true, but one that must be pursued if we would halt the continuing descent of our society from bad to worse. Nothing short of this will suffice. And unless we fully understand the ideal—and what makes for its attainment—we'll tend to settle for powerless, futile little pushes and shoves that yield no more than a false sense of something done.

To grasp the difficulty of the problem as I see it, refer to what the statisticians call a Normal Curve—fat at the middle and thin at either end. Now, represent the adult

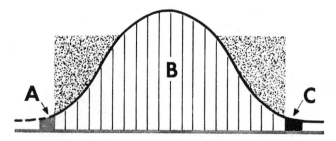

population of the U.S.A. by vertical bands on this curve. Let the thin band at the extreme left (A) symbolize the few articulate, effective protagonists of authoritarianism in its numerous forms. Let the thin band at the extreme right (C) symbolize the few articulate protagonists of individual liberty, the free market economy and its related legal, ethical, and spiritual institutions. Between these two opposed types of intellectuals are the many millions (B), more or less indifferent to this particular problem, as uninterested in understanding the nature of society and its economic and political institutions as are most people in understanding the composition of a symphony. These millions, at best, are only listeners or followers of one intellectual camp or the other. Dr. Ludwig von Mises poses the problem precisely as I see it:

> The masses, the hosts of common men [B], do not conceive any ideas, sound or unsound. They only choose between the ideologies developed by the intellectual leaders of mankind [A or C]. But their choice is final and determines the course of events. If they prefer bad doctrines [A], nothing can prevent disaster.[1]

But, first, who are "the hosts of common men"? Rarely does an individual think of himself as included—only others belong to the masses! There is a great deal of such inaccurate self-appraisal. As related to the problem here in question, any person—be he wealthy or poor, a Ph.D. or unschooled, a political big-wig or voter, a captain of industry or an unskilled worker—qualifies as a member of the

---

[1] *Human Action* (1963 edition. New Haven: Yale University Press), p. 864.

masses if he does "not *conceive* ideas, sound or unsound."
Conversely, wealth or educational or occupational status is
not a controlling factor in determining "the intellectual
leaders of mankind." These leaders are the ones who *conceive* ideas, sound or unsound, and they come from all stations in life. These facts are important to what follows.

Today, the masses (B) are listening to and following the
intellectual leaders at the left (A). The reason is that the
intellectuals at the right (C) have not done and are not
now doing their homework; indeed, most of them have
little inkling of either the need for or the nature of such
homework.

The Spiritual Quality

Many of us who think, write, and speak for freedom—
myself included—have thought that our mission could best
be served by teaching free market economics along with
consistent governmental theory; that is, the disciplines
which have to do with how *man* acts in response to given
situations in society. But this, we are discovering, is not
the whole story. For example, a man lacking in high moral
and spiritual standards can have the libertarian philosophy
"down pat" in the realm of political economy; he can
grade 100 per cent in any test but may, nevertheless, throw
his influence behind collectivism! In such an instance we
have nothing whatsoever to show for our educational pains
—nothing but little pushes and shoves that yield no more
than a false sense of something done.

I know of a top labor official who, like some others, has
learned and can explain the free enterprise philosophy as

skillfully as anyone can. But this man, weak in moral disciplines, disregards his knowledge as he grasps for personal power. The rest of us would be as well off were he an economic illiterate.

The above observation is not to deprecate teachings in the social sciences; far from it! These teachings are a requisite to understanding. Yet, to pin our hopes for a good society on these teachings alone is but to delude ourselves. *What is the moral and spiritual quality of the man who is learning?* This, we are discovering, is the real question; indeed, it is the primary question we must answer, and answer satisfactorily.

I feel that the foregoing is a necessary preface to further probing in an area seldom explored by individuals devoted to economic education. Education in economics and government is important, but this alone will not solve our problem. There is a further need, yes, a necessity, for what Jefferson called "a natural aristocracy among men, founded on virtue and talents." Without this—so will run my argument—economic expertness or sound organizational theories of society will avail us nothing. This is a hard confession for one who has long thought that our country's disastrous trend could be reversed by little more than a return to economic sanity.

Hard to Focus on the Problem

The need for a natural aristocracy is not generally recognized. Why? It may be that most of us are unaware of the relatively undeveloped state in which we as humans now exist. Our unawareness, such as it is, may stem from a failure to put ourselves in proper long-range perspective. In no small measure, this would seem to account for a great deal of unwarranted self-esteem, for thinking of ourselves as the ultimate in perfection, for our egocentricity. Our natural tendency is to regard the universe as something which revolves around each little "me."

No person in such a state of self-satisfaction is in any shape to recognize his incompleteness, let alone to improve, to emerge, to continue the hatching process, to soar into what Jefferson meant by a natural aristocracy. A person who regards himself as a complete specimen of humanity can hardly acquire more virtue and talents. If a natural aristocracy is a requirement, then it follows that most of us need a keener appreciation of our past and present status relative to what we might become.

A slight beginning toward an improved perspective might be gained by comparing the time span of what we call humanity with the time span of that infinitesimal speck in the universe we call earth.[2] For instance, let a 10,000-foot jet runway represent the time span of this planet—perhaps 2,500,000,000 years. So far as the records reveal, Cro-Magnon man put in his appearance 40,000 years ago, less than the last two inches of the 10,000-foot runway! Man—from Cro-Magnon to us—is no more than a Johnny-come-lately!

In what condition did these relatively recent ancestors of ours find themselves? Of knowledge, as we use the term,

---

[2] For a dramatic demonstration of the earth's infinitesimal place in the cosmos, see the drawings of Helmut Wimmer in the April 1959 issue of *Natural History,* or the book, *Cosmic View,* by Kees Boeke, published by the John Day Company in 1957.

it is doubtful if they had any. Science? Philosophy? Art? Religion? We wonder if they knew where they were or who they were. How could they have known the past without any history or tradition? Could they have had any capital, that is, any material or spiritual wealth? Or any inheritance, that is, from the toil of past generations? They must have been without tools, without precedents, without guiding maxims, without speech as we know it, with little if any light of human experience. Their ignorance, as we understand the term, must have been nearly absolute.[3]

The above would seem to be a fair picture of where we were only a few moments ago in long-range time. But where are we now in relation to our destiny? Using human destiny as a yardstick, we have barely moved. According to the scientists, most species require a million years to develop. Should this rule of nature apply to humans, then we have 95 per cent of the way to go in civilizing ourselves—an occasion for humility as well as hope.

Numerous Oversouls

Of course, it is absurd to believe that human beings will upgrade more evenly in the coming eons than in the past 40,000 years. Every species, including the human species, has its throwbacks and its great masses of mediocrity. But, encouragingly, the record is punctuated with numerous

---

[3] A paraphrasing of a statement by the late Cassius Jackson Keyser, mathematician-philosopher of Columbia University and quoted by A. Korzybski in his *Manhood of Humanity* (2nd ed. Lakeville: Institute of General Semantics, 1950), p. 295.

oversouls, "the spirit which inspires and motivates all living things." While many among us show little if any advancement over the original specimens, there have been and are a few who, in some respects, serve as lodestars, as guiding ideals, as models of excellence, as exemplars of the human potential, and thus qualify for what is meant by a natural aristocracy. Further, if the human species makes the grade, instead of falling by the wayside, the unevenness we have noted—the mass of mediocrities and the few oversouls—probably will continue throughout the millennia of man's hoped-for emergence in consciousness, awareness, perception, reason; in man's power to choose and to accomplish what he wills.

The careful observer can hardly help noting certain "breakthroughs" which demonstrate the potential in mankind. Reflect on Jesus of Nazareth. Bear in mind such high specimens of humanness as Hammurabi, Ikhnaton, Ashoka, Guatama Buddha, Lao-tse, Confucius, Moses, Socrates, and, a moment closer to our own time, Beethoven, Milton, Leonardo da Vinci, Goethe, Rembrandt, and so on. Edison, Pasteur, Poincare, Einstein have, in their ways, soared above most of us and given us light. The performances of these uncommon and remarkable persons are but prophecies of what potentially is within the reach of our species.

Whether or not our species will move on toward its destiny or, more to the immediate point, whether or not we, the living, and our children will be able to play our role in and benefit from a human emergence, would seem to depend on what elements in the population predominate.

Will those who are failures in the emerging process rise to political power, forming an inhibiting kakistocracy—a government by the worst men—and thus retard or destroy the process?[4] Or will our course be determined by a natural aristocracy founded on virtue and talents? We, in our times, may well be living in one of the great moments of decision.

One thing seems crystal clear: The worst elements in each one of us will predominate in any moment of time when the aristocratic spirit in each one of us is not "in the pink of condition"; the slightest letdown in its moral, intellectual, and spiritual virility must inevitably witness disaster. This is true in nature: the weeds, pests, fungi, viruses, parasites take over whenever their natural enemies experience a letdown. Virtue and talents, the natural enemies of ignorance, knavery, foolishness, malevolence, must be perpetually flowering to hold these evils in check. This is to suggest that our species will not make the grade in the absence of those emerged spirits which inspire and motivate the human race toward its destiny. Man alone, of all creatures, has been granted the freedom to participate in his own creation.

Conceding the need for a natural aristocracy is one thing, perhaps a first step in right thinking. But more is required than the mere repetition of the virtue and talents of those who have gone before us. If nothing more than carbon copies were required, it then follows that we of

---

[4] "Is ours a government of the people, by the people, for the people or a Kakistocracy rather, for the benefit of knaves at the cost of fools?" —James Russell Lowell.

our generation would exhibit no improvement over Cro-Magnon man. We would have no language, no knowledge; the ignorance that was his would be adequate. No, the human situation is not meant to be static; it has no stopping place, no "this is it!" Instead, it is a dynamic process, the essential requirement of which is perpetual hatching in virtue and talents, an eternal improvement in consciousness, awareness, perceptivity.

Developing Consciousness

No doubt the scientists are correct in claiming that most species take a million years to develop. Humanness, however, is geared not to the finite but to the Infinite and thus, I believe, what applies to other species does not necessarily apply to man. True, man cannot conceive of infinity, even in the case of time and space. But he can become aware of infinity by the simple acknowledgment that he cannot comprehend finite time or space—a point in time or space beyond which there is no more time or space. By the same token, man cannot conceive of infinite consciousness, *consciousness being the singular, distinguishing characteristic of humanness,* but he can become aware of it by admitting that he cannot conceive a level of consciousness beyond which there could be no further refinement of consciousness.

The human situation, it seems, by reason of this peculiar quality of consciousness, is linked to eternity; its design includes no point of retirement; it admits of no Shangri-La implications whatsoever; perpetual struggle and the overcoming of endless confrontations is of its essence. How else can man emerge in consciousness except as he succeeds in overcoming obstacles? Difficulties, problems, hardships do, indeed, have their deep purpose.

This, however, is not to deny that individuals are free to retire, to resign from the climb, to get out of life, to surrender self-responsibility, to think short-range, to "live it up" here and now; they can and do exercise their freedom in this respect, and on the grand scale! And these who acquire so little of that which is distinctly human are assuredly among the many who can and will take over in the absence of a first-rate aristocracy.

It may very well be that a purpose is served by these dropouts from the struggle, among whom are numbered many of the famous, the wealthy, the "educated," and "leaders" in business, church, and state, along with hosts of the nondescript. It is the threat of their take-over, the danger of their dominance of the human situation, that triggers the aristocratic spirit into existence; their actions bring on reactions; their devolution is the genesis of evolution; these agents of disaster are meant to create an antiagency of survival. Without them, the emerging process would cease; for man cannot *become* except as he *overcomes*. A strong position rests on strong opposition.[5] At work here is the tension of the opposites or the law of polarity. In short, the unfortunate quitters serve as springboards to those who pioneer progress.

---

[5] "Compensation" is the word Emerson used. Refer to his essay by this title.

A Responsibility to Create

If every action has its reaction, as observation affirms, some people will conclude that we then have nothing to fret about; in other words, let nature take its course while we spin our own little webs. What is overlooked in such a conclusion is that the human situation is peculiarly distinguished by consciousness, a quality not found in other life forms. And as consciousness emerges, there comes with it a responsibility to share in the creative process. An expansion of the individual's consciousness toward a harmony with Infinite Consciousness demands of the individual that he take on, commensurately, other characteristics of his Creator. It is absurd to believe that there can be any growth in that direction without a corresponding emergence of creativity in man.

True, every action has a reaction but, unless there is a conscious effort—unnatural effort or, better yet, above the natural—to exercise the new creativity born of added consciousness, the reaction to the dominance of ignorance, knavery, and foolishness will take only the form of displeasure, hate, vengeance, cynicism, satire, political bickering, snobbery, name-calling. Clearly, there is no emergent power in this type of reaction, none whatsoever. No natural aristocracy can be born of this. Such reactions are at the same low level as the ignorant, knavish, foolish actions. And, with nothing more than this, ignorance, knavery, foolishness will continue to dominate society.

To summarize the foregoing: It is my belief that those qualities of character which have sufficed to bring progress in the past will prove inadequate from here on; indeed, the mere duplication of past virtue and talents will not stand us in good stead right now. We need, at this juncture in man's emergence, a natural aristocracy of higher quality than has heretofore existed. Looking at the human situation with an emerging perspective permits no other conclusion! The natural aristocracy must be a more distinguished body than ever before, because today's crisis is that much greater. Extraordinary effort must be put forth as a necessary condition to human emergence, or even for survival!

Our Prime Objective

If the above observations are valid, it follows that the establishment of a natural aristocracy should be our prime objective; the teaching of economics or other disciplines of the social sciences can be meaningful only if individuals of virtue and talents are presupposed. What, then, are the qualifications for membership?

Unless careful, we are likely to think of membership in the natural aristocracy as consisting of a set of persons, for such, indeed, has been the case in various so-called aristocracies, composed, as they have been, of privileged minorities possessed of great wealth or social position. Aristocracy, in common usage, has been correctly interpreted as consisting of persons of a certain lineage or legal standing.

But the natural aristocracy, such as we have in mind, is even more exclusive; its membership is distinguished by manifested virtue and talents. It is not based on law or a given parentage; it must be regarded as more than an order of persons because there is no individual who is absolutely virtuous and talented, nor anyone wholly lacking some virtue and talents.

Now and then there is a person who manifests extraordinary virtue and talents, relative, at any rate, to the rest of us. Observing this, we are led into the error of following a fallible individual rather than emulating the virtue and talents he possesses, these being the bench marks of a natural aristocracy. The error is serious. To become a Confucius or a Goethe is impossible, but the virtue of the one and the talents of the other are to some degree attainable and, perhaps by a few, surpassable.

How, then, is the individual to seek identification with the natural aristocracy among men? Strict instruction, I am certain, would deny to anyone the privilege of saying, "I am now a member of the natural aristocracy." Glory and fame for the man would not be permissible, only glory and fame for the virtues and talents—the characteristics rather than the characters!

The individual himself, insofar as he might have any association with this type of aristocracy, would be now in and now out, as virtue and talents showed forth through his actions or were obscured by them. Perhaps we could say that no individual would have any identification with the aristocracy whatsoever except *during those moments when he might be in an improving state.* In this state—such would be the concentration—he would not himself be aware of his own status. Indeed, any feeling of what-a-good-boy-am-I would be a sure sign of exclusion from the aristocracy.

A natural aristocracy, then, does not consist of "aristocrats" as commonly interpreted but, instead, is an aristocratic spirit which might show forth or manifest itself in any serious and determined person. What persons? Hanford Henderson answered the question in this manner:

> He may be a day laborer, an artisan, a shopkeeper, a professional man, a writer, a statesman. It is not a matter of birth, or occupation, or education. It is an attitude of mind carried into daily action, that is to say, a religion. It [the aristocratic spirit] is the disinterested, passionate love of excellence . . . everywhere and in everything; the aristocrat, to deserve the name, must love it in himself, in his own alert mind, in his own illuminated spirit, and he must love it in others; must love it in all human relations and occupations and activities; in all things in earth or sea or sky.[6]

Henderson's statement pretty well stakes out the dimensions of the aristocratic spirit, in essence, the love of excellence which, of course, includes the love of righteousness. And by "disinterested" Henderson meant that this attitude of mind should be for its own sake, without thought of reward in the here or the hereafter.

The love of excellence for its own sake! This is the attitude of mind which, when acquired, witnesses man's sharing in Creation. He becomes, in a sense, his own man.

Indeed, the man who acquires the aristocratic spirit will, quite naturally, have the same viewpoint of economics as does Henry Hazlitt:

---

[6] Excerpted from an article by Hanford Henderson entitled "The Aristocratic Spirit" which appeared as a reprint in *The North American Review*, March, 1920.

> The art of economics consists in looking not merely at the immediate but at the longer effects of any act or policy; it consists in tracing the consequences of that policy not merely for one group but for all groups [universality].

The man with the aristocratic spirit will, along with Immanuel Kant, consider a maxim as good only if this same principle of universality can rationally be applied to it;[7] he will no more be guided by the fear of opprobrium on the part of his fallible fellows than he will by the desire for their approbation. He acts, thinks, and lives in long-range terms, for he has linked himself with eternity by his love of and devotion to excellence.

Imagine, if we can, the enormous difference between the thoughts and actions of laborers, artisans, shopkeepers, professional men, writers, statesmen, as we commonly observe them, and the thoughts and actions of these self-same people were they imbued with the aristocratic spirit!

Suggested Procedures

Let us return now to the Normal Curve, displayed at the beginning of this chapter, and contemplate the task of the few at the right (C). Only through unprecedented excellence on their part can disaster be averted. In our search for an excellence that might attract the millions (B) away from authoritarian leadership (A), I would offer two simple suggestions.

---

[7] If one can rationally concede that every person on earth [universality] has the right to his life, his livelihood, his liberty, then, according to Kant, the maxim is good.

The first concerns humility: Neither we nor anyone else can design or draft or organize a good society. No one person nor any committee can make even a pencil; a good society is more complex than that! A pencil or a good society or whatever is but a benefit or dividend which flows as a consequence of antecedent attention to one's own emergence toward excellence. This thought, a realization of one's limitations, eliminates useless endeavors; it steers one toward the aristocratic spirit; it is the way to qualify.

The second is but a detail that may help in making qualification less difficult: Regardless of the benefit we would have bestowed, always strive for a related goal over and beyond the benefit. The method or principle I have in mind is not new; it was known by the ancients: "But seek ye first the kingdom of God, and his righteousness; and all these things shall be added. unto you." This principle of seeking something higher than the benefit was meant as well for general, day-to-day, earthly application. It is a right principle and, therefore, must work at all levels of endeavor.

For instance, if one desires admiration, do not seek admiration but strive for a behavior that can be admired. If we would be rid of poverty, then offer not handouts but liberty to all. In short, if one's ideal is no higher than the benefit, the pursuit of that ideal, paradoxically, will have no reward in store. A by-product never has its origin in itself, but always in something superior to itself. Capital is the antecedent to a dividend.

If we would have a good society then look not to it, but to excellence in all things—and above all to virtue and integrity in our every deed and thought. The dividend will be as good a society as we deserve.

The ups and downs in society are guided by the rise and fall of the aristocratic spirit, by the unremitting pursuit of excellence. It is utter folly to look for social felicity when this spirit is in the doldrums, and no maneuver less than the passionate pursuit of excellence will matter one whit. The good society, with its open opportunity for individual development—let me repeat—is a dividend we receive when virtue and talents are flowering, when the love of excellence in all things is riding high—even in economics.

I can try to qualify. So can you. This is the way every trend gets its start. Who knows? *We* might start a trend!

INDEX

Prepared by Vernelia A. Crawford

The letter "n" following a figure refers to a footnote.

BOOKS FROM FEE

Prices subject to change. Please add $3.00 per order for shipping and handling.

To order, write or phone:

The Foundation for Economic Education
30 South Broadway
Irvington-on-Hudson, NY 10533
(914) 591-7230; FAX (914) 591-8910